ŒUFS

15

2

6

7

8

9

22

23

Gastronomie!

FOOD MUSEUMS *and*
HERITAGE SITES OF FRANCE

Tom Hughes & Meredith Sayles Hughes

BUNKER HILL PUBLISHING

in association with **The FOOD Museum**

To the memory of Kenneth Hudson,
the initiator of the European Museum Forum and European Museum of the Year Award
and editor of The Directory of World Museums. *An independent thinker who*
thought that museums should truly "muse" upon often-overlooked subjects,
in the early 1970s Mr. Hudson asked the question that started us down the food museum path:
"Of the 25,000 museums in the world, why is there none dedicated to the potato?"

And
To the food-loving people of France.

www.bunkerhillpublishing.com

First published in 2005 by Bunker Hill Publishing Inc.
285 River Road, Piermont, NH 03779 USA

10 9 8 7 6 5 4 3 2 1

Copyright © Meredith Sayles Hughes and Tom Hughes
All rights reserved

ISBN 1 59373 029 2

Designed by Louise Millar
Copyedited by George T. Kosar, Ph.D., The Sarov Press

Printed in China

Contents

Foreword

To eat is a necessity of life. The act of eating binds us to the land every day from birth to death. In the search for food, not only did we invent agriculture and technology, but also created culture and organized society. The history of the world, with its exchange between mankind and nature, is really the story of food, diversity, and cooking.

We are delighted that *Gastronomie!* by Tom Hughes and Meredith Sayles Hughes has captured the beautiful and rich adventure that is food. We welcome this invaluable and pioneering guide to our fellow food museums, food heritage sites and monuments gastronomiques, and wish your readers happy passage to some of the glories of France, one part of our common global food heritage.

Jacques Lefort, President
& Christian Bourdel, Director,
AGROPOLIS MUSEUM,
MONTPELLIER, FRANCE.

Agropolis Museum in Montpellier is at once a living museum,
scientific research center, and community of scholars
focussed on global agriculture, cooking and culture.
www.museum.agropolis.fr

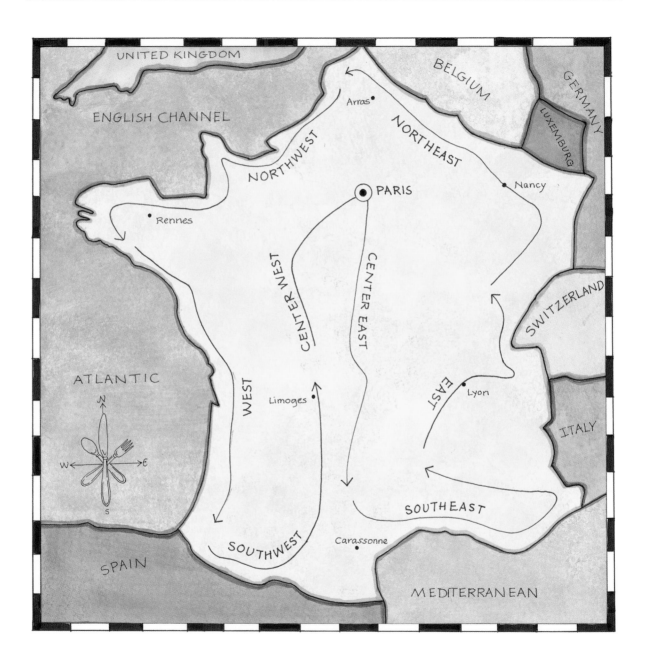

Introduction

"History celebrates the battlefields whereon we meet our death, but scorns to speak of the plowed fields whereby we thrive; it knows the names of the kings' bastards but cannot tell us the origin of wheat. That is the way of human folly."
JEAN-HENRI CASIMIR FABRE, 1823-1915

Dedicated "foodies" will not be surprised to learn that France, considered by many to be the mother country of Western cuisine, is the home of more museums about food, and more initiatives to preserve food heritage traditions and sites, than any other. Food and drink matter to the French, even if they do stop off at the *traiteur* to pick up a moist serving of *ratatouille* and a creamy slab of *pommes de terre dauphinoises*, on a work night. Despite the inroads of fast food, and the presence of "le micro" in many French kitchens, region by region and town by town, people are coming together to preserve and protect the country's food heritage.

Blessed by a country with a diverse yet beneficent climate and 90 percent fertile arable soils, the French have a reverence for "terroir." Inadequately translated as "soil," the word denotes land, even the tastes that specific land gives to food and wine, traditions, and the role of the family in preserving them. Increasingly, however, the majority of frogs, snails, and many other foods associated with French cuisine come from elsewhere. Concerned with what is either lost or in danger of disappearing, motivated people have created the food museums and heritage sites of France—dedicated to researching, collecting, preserving, and explaining the rich diversity of French food and cuisine.

A food museum is a museum about food, pure and simple.

Museums about food are a relatively new museum category, one generally overlooked by traditional guidebooks—we know, we've looked through dozens of them—and yet travelers' interest in food history and traditions is clearly on the rise. The people behind The FOOD Museum, www.foodmuseum.com, we have set out to track down and chronicle the world's museums and sites dedicated to what people eat and drink.

We are not out to determine what makes something called a museum technically legitimate. Our purpose is to pinpoint places that illuminate food history for you the reader, as well as for ourselves. We are after the spirit of inquiry and enthusiasm for a subject, for the places that not only preserve the past but also bring it to life.

This the museums and heritage sites chosen for this book decidedly do. They include professional academically accredited institutions, avowedly commercial public relations ventures, earnestly unsophisticated operations, and variations on all three. Whether called a *musée* or a *maison*, whether a business, marketplace, farm, chateau, or garden, many also offer what most traditional museums do not—the *dégustation* beloved to any food-focused traveler. After experiencing your food history lesson, you can almost always expect an invitation to sample wine, cognac, liqueur, or cider, or taste cheese, pâté, prunes, honey, nuts, tapenade, jams, oils, or ham.

We have not been able to include all the sites we discovered, and undoubtedly have missed many more that could have found a place in this book. We welcome suggestions from you about the French food museums and heritage sites you have experienced and enjoyed. Visit www.foodmuseum.com and click on *Gastronomie!* to add your comments.

In France, foods are labeled and sites are honored.

French officialdom has seriously supported its citizens' inclination to promote food traditions. It has done this through a many-leveled and layered system of labels such as **Label Rouge**, **AOC**, and **IGP**, but also via a relatively recent combined initiative of the Ministers of Culture, Agriculture, and Tourism, known as **Les Sites Remarquables du Goût**.

Labeling to maintain standards, and protect food origins, goes way back in France. People pay more for products carrying the coveted **Label Rouge**, which is a guarantee of superior quality "directly perceptible" to the consumer. **AOC**, or *appellation d'origine contrôlée*, assures that a product comes from a strictly defined geographic region and that it meets the strictest standards of quality.

The **IGP** label, *Indication Géographique Protégée*, states that a product originates from one region and that it has some definite characteristic derived from that regional origin.

Les Sites Remarquables du Goût or Sites of Exceptional Taste recognizes places and institutions that perpetuate France's culinary heritage. All sites must meet three primary criteria. One, they must have an ongoing food production or processing aspect. Two, they must have aesthetic interest, such as beautiful architecture or appealing landscaping. Three, they must allow accessibility to visitors more or less year-round. Places receiving this recognition often post a plaque from *Sites* at their entrances.

Slow Food—Reverence and resistance

"Food history is as important as a baroque church. Governments should recognize this cultural heritage and protect traditional foods. A cheese is as worthy of preserving as a 16th c. building."
CARLO PETRINI, Slow Food Founder

To be at home in the world is to believe that no one is a stranger. By taking time to break bread in harmony with others, by preparing food with care and generosity, we all can glory in the ingredients the planet provides.

Slow Food is "a movement for the protection of the right to taste." Begun in Italy in 1986, established internationally in France in 1989, the Slow Food cause now has over 60,000 members worldwide, and thousands of adherents beyond that. The group's logo is the snail, the deliberate mollusk who moves quietly and smoothly over the garden path, carrying home on its back. In 1607 Italy's Francesco Angelita of L'Aquila wrote a book all about this small creature. In it he wrote that the snail is "of slow motion, to educate us that being fast makes man inconsiderate and foolish" and that "wherever the Snail is, that is its home."

Jose Bové, an "eco-gastronome" and Slow Food advocate who brought McDonald's to a halt, at least for a while, in Millau, rages against what he sees as threats to French food and traditions—genetically modified crops, fast food chains, industrial agriculture practices, importation of many foodstuffs that once were grown locally, mad cow disease, and more. In a quieter way, the many people and communities who create and maintain food museums and food history preservation efforts in France are reverent towards the past, open to change, but resistant to the excesses of modern food production.

Tracking the Tales Behind the Tastes

"First we eat, then we do everything else."
MFK Fisher

Our foodie pilgrimage across France, beginning and ending in Paris, took us six and a half weeks. Unlike the pilgrims of old, we drove rather than walked our 10,000 kilometers, and while the pilgrims were fueled with bread and water, we sampled oysters, drank champagne, and dove into chicken cooked in cream and morels. The scallop shell that became the symbol of religious pilgrimages united them and us—our Renault pulled up to the sign of the shell with great frequency.

As pilgrims do, we have our tales to tell. We exulted upon seeing that a roadside fig seller had faded 1950s advertising materials tacked on the wall. When we stopped for coffee on the autoroutes we were delighted to discover that many *aires* had mounted remarkable exhibits, some featuring food, for travelers assumed to be eager to stretch their minds, as well as their legs.

We doff our caps to the warm, generous people we met all over France—a special *merci* to you, tourism ladies—locally growing, regionally cooking, daily baking, all working to maintain and explain their country's food traditions.

Our journey unfolds in stages, thirty-five of them, in typical pilgrimage style, spread across eight broad geographic areas. Many French people think of their country as a hexagon, with three sides to the sea, two to mountainous borders, and one side running along an open border with Germany, Luxemburg and Belgium. We have included these six sides and added two more areas, dividing the heart of the country into Center East and Center West.

Each entry is identified by department and town. Be warned: France's central government created regional and departmental names in order to have more political and administrative control over the country. The names are confusing. Most French people disregard them and stick to their historic regional names, such as Périgord, known to the English as the Dordogne. Many of the old names turn up as sub-departments, and some actually no longer exist officially.

BBC food reporter Glynn Christian explains this situation well in his marvelous book, *Edible France*.

"It was to Gascony that I wanted to go, but to find Gascony these days needs determination and the very oldest map you can lay hands on. Officially it doesn't exist; and neither do the Quercy, the Rouergue, and Comté de Foix, and other places which people live in, and talk about, and travel to and from. They've all become part of modern *départements*. Thus once you determine where Gascony might be, you find it spilling into all kinds of administratively untidy areas, into Aquitaine in the west and the Languedoc in the east..."

Center East:
Paris, Île de France, Centre, Auvergne-Midi-Pyrénées

Paris is the center of French power, culture, and wealth, its economic muscle secured in the nineteenth century by prodigious harvests of wheat and sugar beets raised in its lush northern plains. But beyond Paris the traveler discovers a region renowned for moldy cheese, accidental apple tart, and a garlicky potato and cheese dish that looks like taffy—an area clearly making the most of what it produces, even if its land is not the most blessed.

Trying to track down someone in Boynes to open the very first food museum on our list, we walked into the local cafe. There we met Jose Manuel Farinha, a Portuguese laborer who has lived in France for twenty years, who welcomed us with coffees, cajoled the cafe owner into phoning the Saffron Museum guide, and then waited for us after the visit, with a perfectly chilled bottle of champagne. A rough region perhaps, but one that treats its guests generously.

Auvergne is not wine country—it turns out bitter yellowy liqueurs, derived from the lemon-flowered mountain meadow plant, *Gentiana lutea*, warming drinks that perfectly suit its brisk climate. Lentils grown in volcanic rock soil fill up empty stomachs here, enriched with pork, the animal of choice honored in a tiny museum in a hilltop village. This is the eastern heart of France where labor-intensive, highly expensive saffron production once occupied the women of Boynes, while down the road in Milly, mint, the plant that grows itself, was an easy cash crop.

It's also the locale of *pounti*, a dish that mixes pork, chard, herbs, and dried plums into its own distinct Auvergne pâté. Picture a rugged farm woman down to her last few ingredients, with a full house to feed, combining some bits of pork with the last of the Swiss chard in the garden, grabbing a jar of preserved plums, and tossing it all together with an egg or two, some flour, and pinches of dried tarragon. That's *pounti*, leftovers elevated to regional specialty.

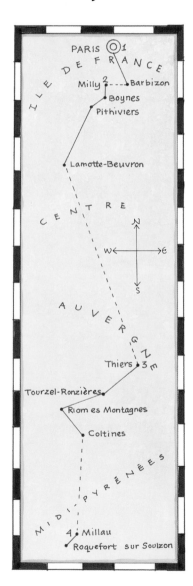

Stage 1: Paris to Barbizon

We'll always have Paris, and the pomme de terre

If we start our pilgrimage in Paris with the potato, it's because the *pomme de terre* is near and dear to our hearts. We got our start in food history with the noble tuber, living in another foodie capital, Brussels, back in 1975. Researching the world's most important vegetable, a food plant that truly influenced history, we began collecting, writing, and teaching about food and its historic roots and global ramifications.

The potato is native to the Americas, to the Andes Mountains, and the colorful story of its travels is well told elsewhere. Its influence on France has been immense—starting out as a devil-tainted underground food foisted on the poor (it was first tried out on hapless hospital patients in Seville), then sampled and enjoyed in the soup kitchens of A.A. Parmentier, it became a prime ingredient in French cooking and remains so today.

Antoine Auguste Parmentier (1737-1813), an apothecary who became a vigorous promoter of the American potato in France, first met the tuber as a prisoner of war in Hanover, Germany, during the Seven Years War. Later as the army's chief apothecary he worked to improve the nutrition of his soldiers, as well as their hygiene. In order to convince the people of France as to the taste and nutritional benefits of the potato, Parmentier established soup kitchens for the poor, ladeling out his version of potato leek soup, known from then on as *potage Parmentier*. Parmentier was a fan of Napoleon, seeing in him a leader (dictator?) who could best convince the people to improve their diets.

Arms maker Pierre-Frédéric Dorian caricatured as a potato head by Alfred Petit in 1871, one plant in his series Le Potager Republicain.

Parmentier's and Millet's pomme de terre

The **Parmentier Metro** stop in the northeastern section of Paris near Place de la République (11eme) is a mini homage to the renowned chemist. Well-lighted cases reveal the history of the potato as well as Parmentier's life work—between the cases is a downsized copy of the statue in Parmentier's northeastern home of Montdidier showing the chemist handing a soon-to-be-fabled tuber to a farmer.

Note: Should you pass through Montdidier, look for shops selling an almond paste candy in the shape of a potato—*la pomme de terre de Montdidier* was created in 1962 to honor the potato and give a public relations boost to the community. **Confiserie Beslard** in Montdidier lays claim to its creation, but the candy is found in many of the town's confiseries.

Metro Parmentier to Père Lachaise

You can cut across Paris from west to east on Line 3, Galieni to Pont de Levallois, and take in both Parmentier's life and his final resting place, getting off at Metro Père Lachaise. In **Père Lachaise**, the cemetery of the famous, potato promoter Parmentier lies next to the satirical playwright Molière, for whom Parmesan cheese was the food of choice. In his later years he lived on port and cheese, and the diet did not needlessly prolong his life. He passed away at age 51, shortly after portraying a hypochondriac in his own play, *The Imaginary Invalid*. Parmentier fared better with the potato, surpassing Molière by twenty-five years.

Hôtel des Invalides

Parmentier's first scientific labs were set up on these elegant floors, to aid his studies as the Army's chief apothecary. In 1772 he published his "Examination of the Chemistry of Potatoes," a work that won him the top prize in a competition seeking a food that could stand in for wheat in times of famine. (In recent years it was still possible to view an exhibition about his labs.)

Les Sablons, Neuilly sur Seine

In order to persuade farmers and gardeners to plant potatoes, Parmentier cajoled Louis XVI, who was already fond of wearing potato flowers in his buttonhole, to allow a planting of potatoes in a field owned by the military, **Les Sablons**. Parmentier posted guards there every day, all day, but sent them home at night. The locals quickly decided that a highly desirable crop was being guarded, and soon were digging up spuds and carrying them away.

Les Sablons is a park today. You can view it, as well as the mural depicting Parmentier, Louis XVI, and the potato field on view at the Mairie. A statue of Parmentier stands out front.

Commissioned by an American, Millet's painting The Angelus, *was finished in 1857. Its earliest name was* Prayer for the Potato Crop. *(Early 1900s postcard.)*

Maison-Atelier, J.F. Millet, Barbizon

Jean-François Millet, one of the artists of the Barbizon school and the famed painter of numerous agricultural scenes such as *The Gleaners* and *The Angelus*, never worked outdoors. All of his art was created in his *atelier* on the quaint main street of the village of Barbizon. You can visit this crowded studio, virtually unchanged from when he worked there from 1849 to 1875. He died in a small room upstairs, not generally open to the public.

This same room now houses a private, amusing, and exceedingly eclectic collection about Millet's *The Angelus*, a painting once dubbed "the most famous in the world." Originally titled "Prayer for the Potato Crop," *The Angelus* shows a man and a woman standing in a field, heads bowed in evening prayer over a basket of potatoes. This image has become as lampooned and reinterpreted as Grant Woods' Iowa classic, *American Gothic*. Anne Marie Meunier, owner of the Millet property, and her late husband, Jacques, a travel writer, "collected Angelus items without much searching—they are everywhere." The small room is packed with Angelus memorabilia and *tchatchkes*: needlepoint Angelus pillows for cat baskets, chocolate molds, advertising materials promoting a bookstore, and assorted reinterpretations of the image in oils, including her husband's favorite, a painting of the Angelus couple rendered as his-and-her tobacco pipes—and still more. If you profess to a sincere foodie interest in Millet and this painting, you may be invited upstairs. (To see the actual Angelus you must visit the **Musée d'Orsay**, 1 rue de la Légion d'Honneur, in Paris.)

Auvergne's green lentils, grown in rich, volcanic soil, and often perfectly paired with pork, garlic, and onion, have garnered the AOC classification. This agricultural area employs 15 percent of the working population and produces a whopping 60% of France's lentils.

Aligot, like a tasty chewing gum that you're allowed to swallow. It is garlic mashed potatoes with a cheesy feel. It's made fresh with local Cantal cheese and can be an entire meal, especially if taken with a decent green salad. And by the way, it's a mountain food and is fun to fool with—you can play with it like taffy.

13

Stage 2: Milly to Boynes to Pithiviers to Lamotte-Beuvron

In Milly, mint is the taste of choice, while subtle saffron rules in Boynes. **Le Musée du Safran** (aka Maison du Safran) typifies the finest qualities of the food museums and heritage sites of France, offering an impeccable, well-cared-for collection that effectively, step-by-step tells the story of a local food. But save your appetite for two cakes, regional stars that have gone national: the Pithiviers *fondant glacé*, and the oozing apple extravaganza, *Tarte Tatin*.

La Halle, Milly la Forêt
The forty-eight chestnut wood pillars of the handsome market hall in Milly la Forêt have been holding up the graceful, timbered roof that has sheltered food purveyors every year since its construction in 1479. Vendors of the famous locally grown mint, watercress grown since the nineteenth century in nearby Méréville, many medicinal herbs, and the usual fruits, vegetables, and meats, come together here every Thursday afternoon, Milly's market day. You can also buy mint and mint products at the local **Milly Menthe** shop right on the main street.

Musée du Safran, Boynes
"The more one trods on the saffron, the more it blooms.
So it is with the grandeur of France: the more it is trampled on, the more it grows."

Pierre Ronsard, 1524–1585

The museum's high-ceilinged, whitewashed stone building, formerly housing a wine merchant's business, beautifully shows off the museum's holdings. Curator Pierre Templier is a retired farmer who volunteers for the commune as a guide, and he knows his subject well.

The exotic "red gold" that is saffron is no longer the prime occupation of the women of Boynes, but at its peak in the late nineteenth century the saffron business employed all the able women of the town, current population just over 1,000, and its products were known throughout Europe. In October at harvest time, workers gathered the lavender-hued crocus flowers into uniquely shaped gathering baskets on display here—they are wide, with closed-off ends to keep the wind from blowing them away.

A petite iron stove, over which dangles a wooden sieve with a fine mesh, was used to dry the stigma by hand, "just exactly the right length of time," according to M. Templier. Too much heat and the saffron loses its flavor. Too little drying and it becomes moldy. French saffron growers, unlike the Spanish, did not have the luxury of sun-drying their products.

Whether introduced into France by the Crusaders returning from the Holy Land, or brought across the border from Spain with the Moors, saffron was being cultivated throughout southern France by the fourteenth century. The exotic product was used to flavor liqueurs, dye clothing a deeply satisfying yellow, color assorted dishes, and aid ailments of the heart, stomach, and lungs. By the end of the fifteenth century, the French saffron industry was thriving, stealing business away from its rival, Spain.

A note on Pâté d'Alouette

Remember the lovely little ditty, "Alouette, gentille alouette?" It refers to the plucking of the presumably dead songbird, prior to cooking and preparing it in such dishes as pâté d'alouette, a recipe for which begins: "Pluck, clean, and singe a dozen larks..." When he was twenty years old, M. Templier made his own lark net that now stretches across the ceiling in one room of the saffron museum. The instrument of the lark's destruction, reminding us of Narcissus' pool, was a cleverly designed, twirling wooden wing-shaped device, covered in small mirrors or shiny reflective circles (look for them in the small glass display case). It was placed above the wide net and the birds, lured by the dazzling things, presumably arrived in droves to investigate. "There was a time," explained M. Templier, when there was not always so much to eat." Lark hunting has long been outlawed in France.

An offbeat favorite is *faux safran*, sold by unscrupulous vendors—unwary cooks may have sprinkled powdered red brick or dried cut corn silk on their food.

When the market for French saffron collapsed after the Great War, with Spain gaining ground as a supplier, farmers began growing potatoes, beets, and finally wheat in their fields. The courtyard of the museum displays fine examples of early machines used for these crops on either side of its main path.

The origins of the Pithiviers cake, a frosted concoction of layered pastry and almonds, date so far back they are hard to trace. But its distinctive topping of preserved fruits has been around since the eighteenth century. Most of the bakeries in town offer this treat, some with the white glazed frosting, some more plain, both worth a trip.

15

Hôtel-Restaurant Tatin, Lamotte Beuvron

Ardent pilgrims in search of the home of the famous *Tarte Tatin*, we arrived at the **Hôtel-Restaurant Tatin** in Lamotte Beuvron about 8:00 in the evening on February 14, utterly oblivious to the date and its possible significance, though it was indeed a Saturday night. The dining room was jammed, there was absolutely no possibility of dining there, but yes, they would show us the famous upside-down caramelized apple tart. One was held discreetly under our noses, just long enough for us to say "ah!" and then whisked off to a sideboard for serving. Rule Two of the *Tarte Tatin*—it must be eaten hot from the oven, a dictate derived from Rule One, a genuine *Tarte Tatin* must be ordered with one's dinner.

Stories differ as to the origins of this delectable dessert. In 1888 two sisters, Stephanie and Caroline, took over the running of the hotel from their father. According to one story, Stephanie, the cook, was adept at making apple tarts but one day, in the mad rush of feeding guests at hunting season, she prepared the tart backwards, putting the apples in the dish first. Another story implies that she had cooked tarts on the stove top all along, having no oven. Yet another story relates that Stephanie was flirting with a customer, having just put some apples and butter and sugar on the stove to cook, and rushed to the kitchen to find them darkened and caramelized. The resourceful Stephanie tried to salvage them by putting pastry on top, thereby creating dessert history.

Tarte Tatin

The piece we ate, in the car with our fingers (momentarily parted from our picnic gear and unwilling to wait), was warm, and meltingly delicious.

Fill a 10-inch-deep flame-safe pie dish with a good deal of unsalted butter, about $1^1/2$ cups. Sprinkle about $1^1/2$ cups confectioner's sugar in the butter.

Peel about 2 pounds of tart apples, cut them roughly into quarters, and place them side by side, curved side down, filling in the gaps with large slices.

Place dish on a low flame and cook for 10-15 minutes, until mix begins to caramelize. Then put in oven at 400 degrees and bake for about $1/4$ hour.

Cut together the following ingredients for a flaky pastry:
1 cup unbleached all purpose flour
8 tablespoons unsalted butter
$1/4$ cup sugar
3 eggs, beaten
2 teaspoons water

Roll dough out somewhat larger than the mold, and place on top of the apples. Bake another $1/4$ hour.
Pull pan from oven and let stand for a few minutes. Place a serving dish over the mold and turn out quickly. Serve immediately.

Recipe courtesy www.tarte-tatin.com.

Stage 3: Thiers to Tourzel-Ronzières to Riom es Montagnes to Coltines

To butcher a pig, you need a knife. As you butcher the pig, you honor him. And to fully enjoy his meat, you need some nutty-tasting lentils, well-seasoned potatoes, and to start the meal off right, a mountain *gentian* aperitif.

La Coutellerie de Laguiole, Thiers

Chances are good, if you have used a knife in France, it came from Laguiole and featured the bee symbol on its shaft. (Or is it a fly, a reference to the flies encountered by knife-wielding cow herders in the region? Experts disagree.) You can visit the *atelier* where 50,000 knives are produced each year, and you can also tour the museum that tells the history of both the company, begun in 1829, and the knife itself.

Petit Musée de la Cochonaille, Tourzel-Ronzières

"What an admirable animal," wrote Jules Renard of the pig. "He lacks only the know how to make his own sausage." The man who guided us to this small permanent exhibit about pig butchery had just returned from deer hunting, his tall green boots muddy and his bright orange hat askew. He tipped his hat to us, and to the glorious *cochon*, as he put it, declaring that he had been a butcher's apprentice to his grandfather at the age of sixteen.

Inside the whitewashed building belonging to the commune—it's always open, and the light switch is on the wall—the pig is honored in poetry, old photos, and unpleasant-looking tools, as well as a *baillard* or ladder of sorts from which the honored beast was hung to bleed, dare we say.

The feast of Saint Cochon was always celebrated by the roasting of five to six pigs, in a village the size of Tourzel, he told us. As we were leaving he suddenly pulled his shirt off, revealing a tattoo of a *sanglier* or wild boar.

LE TOUR DU COCHON.......

17

Maison de la Gentiane, Riom es Montagnes

Bitters such as the French brand Suze are made from the root of the yellow *Gentiana lutea*, a tall perennial herb. You can get to know the five hundred species of gentian here, walk through the maison's botanical garden, observe the making of gentian aperitifs, and, yes, do some tasting.

Musée de l'Agriculture d'Auvergne—L'Ostal de le Marissou, Coltines

The four seasons by which the people of Auvergne once closely lived are beautifully expressed in this fine farming museum, set in a handsome restored seventeenth-century stone farm building. The focus is on the basics—grain growing, cheese making, oxen and sheep petting, it's all here.

Stage 4: Roquefort sur Soulzon to Millau

In a "land where neither vineyard nor corn can grow," it makes sense to go for the cheese. And little is as fine as a creamy, salty bite of Roquefort, atop half a fresh fig. One of the suppliers of milk to Roquefort cheese makers, Jose Bové woke up to the inroads of globalization on French traditions when the US slapped high tariffs on his beloved cheese.

Société Roquefort, Roquefort

First mentioned in the eighteenth century, Roquefort cheese had its AOC label by 1925, and along with champagne was said to be the most famous product of France. The fine milk of the Lacaune ewes makes it possible, with the help of mold spores known as *penicillium*. Each new cheese is poked in about forty places and then placed unwrapped in a cave. For two to three weeks the cheese is invaded by the greenish-blue spores. After being wrapped, the cheese is then cured until maturity, for a minimum of three months. (Legend speaks of the lustful shepherd who left his cheese in a cave and ran off in pursuit of his lady love. When he finally returned, Mother Nature had transformed his hunk of ewe's milk into Roquefort.)

You can visit the caves year-round, but from June until January you'll see fake plastic cheeses waiting patiently to mature. The real cheese is in place from January to June. The locals will tell you each cave's microclimate has a different character—based on temperature, humidity levels, and air circulation—that produces a slight variation in different Roquefort Cheese products. Taste for yourself.

McDonald's, Millau

Jose Bové became an instant celebrity at the end of the 1990s for taking on both McDonald's, provider of what Bové called "la malbouffe Americaine," "American crappy food," and genetically engineered foods. A steep US tariff on French standards such as *foie gras* and Roquefort has continued to fuel Bové's protests. You can stop by this McDonald's that felt the wrath of Bové even before it opened, but you will see no plaque marking the day he and his followers dismantled the place and dumped its parts on the grass in front of City Hall. Bové was jailed three months for "criminal damages." The McDonald's was swiftly rebuilt, yet Bové's revolution continues. Opposed to the globalization of food as well as the decline in French local foodways, Bové is the author of *The World is Not for Sale*.

As you wolf down your Big Mac, or not, step outside for a view of the highest viaduct in the world, taller than the Eiffel Tower, and the fine vista beyond.

Southeast:
Languedoc-Roussillon, Provence-Côte d'Azur
The provender of Provence

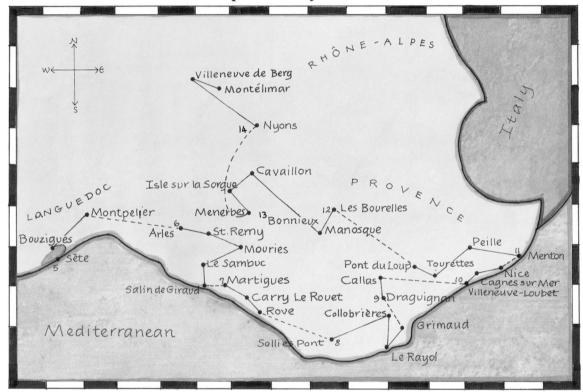

Years ago, when we lived in Belgium, after nine long months of unvarying gray skies, in March we drove straight south in our flaming red Citroen 2cv. When we finally reached the sun, just on the edges of Provence, we pulled over to the side of the road, shot from the car, and danced like deranged inmates, waving our hands in the sunbeams and hooting with delight. Provence may not always have this effect on everyone but its sunny, seductive offerings of rosé wine, mimosa-topped goat cheeses, olives and oils, crystallized lavender and violets, *bouillabaisse*, seafood of every description, *ratatouille*, melons, and asparagus have long drawn Brits and northern Europeans here. This Mediterranean area's hot dry summers and mild wet winters suit evacuees from the north as much as the resident goats, sheep, olive trees, and specialty crops—the Var area is France's largest truffle-growing region.

The Greeks first planted the grapevines and olive trees that thrived in the hot, dry soils. And the Romans who followed them spread wine making throughout the region. The Saracens also nibbled away at these shores, bringers of rice and possibly suppliers of the lemons that later made Menton the home of the annual Lemon Festival.

Even with all this natural bounty, the region has known severe poverty. For many generations, dinner was olive oil and crushed olives on bread. Many of Nice's dishes reflect what poor, famine-plagued people cooked and ate for generations. They traded olive oil for fish and turned salt cod into stew. They ate brown bread, not refined white, and combined chard and yellow raisins to make a filling dessert.

ABOVE: *Salt cod on display at Nice's market.*
RIGHT: *Vegetable tart made from Swiss chard makes a savory dessert*

21

Stage 5: Sète to Bouzigues to Montpellier

Octopus pie, Sète's portable food, is a good introduction to the exotic waters of the south—you'll be looking over your shoulder for the Phoenicians. And the local story of oysters and mussels is captured in the seafood museum of its neighboring town, Bouzigues.

Seafood, and all other food, is further explained in a true world food museum, **Agropolis**, up in the hillside of Montpellier.

Tielles of Sète

Considerable are the charms of Sète, a port city on the Mediterranean with the light and rhythm of Venice. Indeed half the population of Sète is Italian in origin, including Adrienne Verducci, the woman credited with inventing, or at least being the first to sell commercially, Sète's empanada-like specialty, *tielle*, in 1937. These are small pies, portable foods long favored by fishermen, made of hearty bread pastry and filled with tomato sauce, herbs, and octopus. The first heavily oreganoed bite says pizza, but the chewy yet satisfying pieces of *poulpe* (octopus) and the yellow red dough are all *tielle*. Adrienne's descendants sell the *tielles* from **Tielles Cianni** at the bottom of rue Paul Valery, but you can also find them at the daily Sète indoor morning market. Here old meets new—the concrete floor is painted red, new orange tiles climb the walls, the cement beams have been painted, and flat fluorescent lighting hanging over some vendor stalls gives way to theatrical pinspots that make the impossibly fresh blue and purple and red-hued fish sparkle.

Tielles: *Octopus Pies*

Portable food, perhaps this is the "pasty" of France. The pasty, a crimped-edge portable meat pie, provided a handle for the soiled hands of hungry Cornish miners. Perhaps *tielles* were intended to do the same for the tar-and-bait-handed fishermen of Sète.

Serves 4

3/4 c. flour	1 egg
3 1/2 T. butter	1 T. sugar
1 lb. octopus	salt and pepper
2 tomatoes	pinch of cayenne
1 onion	1 T. flour
2 garlic cloves	1 glass white wine
1 T. chopped parsley	1 egg yolk

Mix together flour, butter, egg, sugar, and a pinch of salt, and also add in half a glass of wine. Knead dough lightly on a floured board and then let dough sit, in a cool spot, for about 2 hours. Cut octopus into long, thin pieces. Boil them briefly in salted water. Then sauté them in butter or olive oil with minced garlic and chopped onion. Mix together the tablespoon of flour with the rest of the wine. Add chopped peeled tomatoes, chopped parsley, salt, pepper, and a dash of cayenne. Cook this mixture on low heat for about 40 minutes. Heat oven to 400 degrees. Grease 4 oven-proof custard cups or small soufflé molds and put a fairly thick layer of dough in the bottom of each. Add octopus mix almost to the top, then place a cap of dough on top. Alternatively, take a deep dish pie plate and create one large *tielle*. Pinch together the top layer of dough with the bottom layer. Paint the dough with egg yolk. Place in hot oven and bake for 30 minutes.

Courtesy "Recettes de Languedoc-Roussilon par Stephanie," www.philagora.org

Musée de l'Etang de Thau, Bouzigues

Your major decision in Bouzigues will be whether to eat the delectable local oysters or mussels before or after educating yourself about ostreiculture and mytiliculture at the museum.

Appropriately sited at the eastern corner of the nineteen-kilometer-long lagoon or *"etang,"* with small outboards tied up in front of the door (you can visit the museum by boat from Sète, Meze, or Balaruc-les-Bains, and if the tide is right, see the oyster beds under cultivation), the museum presents the story of the farmed oysters and mussels, the people who produce them, and the local fish of the region, many swimming around in tanks. This is no dusty display-case natural history exhibit, though the history of fishing gear from 1925 to the present may be too much for all but the most ardent fisher. You enter the museum through a tunnel of nets and as you progress, several areas light up as a narrator's voice explains the scene. This technique cleverly brings life to the artifact-driven displays. One section features the voices of fishermen reminiscing about the old days, when there was a small cutout in every fisherman's shack for the faithful cat who would not only clean the nets of any edible fish bits, but also keep the rats at bay.

A spotlighted item is a perfectly maintained example of the graceful flatbottomed *"nacelle,"* which could either sail or be rowed in the shallow *etang* waters and easily be moored anywhere along the shore.

Local winegrowers used rot-proof wood imported from Cameroon, then a French colony, for staking the vines that grew near the shores of the lagoon. When the farmers turned to oyster raising, they chose these *"tiges de bois"* for use in the oyster beds, gluing baby oysters or sprat to the wood before lowering it into the water. Today the oysters grow on plastic ropes, the replacement for the hemp ropes that were also tried.

The museum provides an English text translation of most of the exhibits. A small gift shop in the lobby sells t-shirts, blue smocks, books, cards, shell boxes, and so on.

A string of appealing small restaurants lines the waterfront near the museum. We chose *Chez Francine*, with its bright blue painted ceiling beams, run by the de Blanchards who are oyster producers, not just restaurant owners. We feasted simply but happily on fresh oysters, grilled sardines, and a pitcher of the local crisp white wine, as we watched the lights of Sète coming on.

Agropolis, Montpellier

The Agropolis Museum is *the* food museum of France, and the most exciting and comprehensive museum about food we know of anywhere. Dedicated to describing the global story of people, food, and agriculture, it deftly combines solid information with exceedingly imaginative, inviting displays. Unlike many museums today that rely almost entirely on oversized graphics, Agropolis combines actual artifacts with multimedia. Agropolis goes right at the central role food plays in life, honors those who deliver and cook food, and does not neglect those whose major role is in the eating.

Here you can walk the history of early food gathering and agriculture, and see lively mini exhibits of many of the world's fruits, vegetables, and animals. You can meet eight farmers from around the world, peer into their homes, and hear their stories on video.

Another exhibition on display recreates world food and drink preparations—for example, the tea ceremony in Japan, pasta making in Italy, and coffee rituals in Ethiopia. A voyeur's delight, you look right into a life-size corner of a fully realized room from which the family has just stepped away.

The animation and audiovisual offerings at Agropolis are numerous and changing—two recent *animations* tell the story of grains in ancient Egypt, as well as bread making in Egypt today. This exhibit is available online, as are virtual versions of the museum's three primary permanent exhibitions. The English version is available here: http://museum.agropolis.fr/english/index.html.

At the core of the building is a permanent sculptural exhibition called *The Banquet of Humanity*, or *The Dining Table of the World*, a creation so powerful it silenced the idle buzz of visitors every time we ventured into it. Eight couples sit at a round table set in furrowed ground. At the center is water and, perched atop the water,

Planet Earth. The couples represent three poor countries, three average income countries, and two rich—the rich are Japan and France, the poorest is Somalia. Calories eaten per adult per day in France—3,632. Somalia—1,600.

Outside the circle is another couple, utterly excluded from the table. They are naked—the woman reaches out a hand as if in cooperation, the man holds up his fist in protest. This powerful work by Henri Rouvières goes to the heart of Agropolis' chief focus—despite all scientific advances, money, and effort, world hunger remains a battle not yet won.

Agropolis provides numerous innovative programs and activities for children. French school children can participate in *La Petite École du Goût*, a cooking and tasting class. The museum operates a book shop with Agropolis publications as well as books on assorted food subjects, mostly in French.

A kitchen from Mexico appears opposite that of a Moroccan household

Musée du Bonbon Haribo, Uzes

Haribo is the German candy giant most credited with inventing the first "gummi bears," a product that began in the 1920s and has been imitated and spun off ever since. In 1996 Haribo France opened the global company's first confectionery museum. Housed on three floors, the Bonbon museum explains all facets of candy making, and then lures visitors into a tasting area that neatly segues into the buying area. Not for those lacking will power.

Association Kokopelli, Ales,

is a seed saver organization that promotes biodiversity by distributing heirloom seeds. It is creating a network of gardeners involved in seed saving, and also is helping Third World countries to develop sustainable organic agriculture. Its directory of 2,500 plant varieties includes over six hundred tomatoes, fifty varieties of eggplant, 370 sweet and hot peppers, two hundred squashes, fifty melons, 130 varieties of lettuces, and more.

ABOVE: *Kokopelli seeds produced these heirloom tomato varieties*

BELOW: *The Dining Table of the World, Agropolis.*

Stage 6: Arles, Roman Barbegal, Glanum (St. Rémy) to Mouriès to Salin de Giraud

The first large Roman foothold in Gaul, Arles was soon being called "the little Rome of the Gauls." The citizens of Arles seem to have been an orderly, well-fed people with a cuisine based on wine, wheat, and olives, all still evident in these parts today.

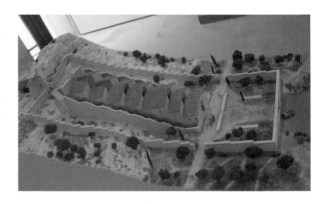

Not part of the area's Roman heritage is rice, brought by the Arabs, and still thriving in the Camargue. This marshy delta region, originally a malaria-infested, salt-encrusted, many-branched wilderness populated mainly by French cowboys and their cattle, was created where the Rhône river flows into the Mediterranean. The first domestic rice was grown here to help desalinate the land for wheat planting.

The unique local rice is known as Red Rice of the Camargue, a creation of nature—a melding of the wild-growing, red-headed rice and a domesticated white rice only dating back to the 1980s. You can learn more about it at the **Rice Museum**, and sample it in French *paella* at the Arles regional **Rice Festival**.

Musée de l'Arles et de la Provence

At first glance, this magnificent museum about Roman Arles, set right on the Rhône River, does not seem like a foodie destination, until you discover what's inside, such as the *Daily Life* section, which displays cups, bowls, casserole dishes, bronze kettles, bottles, goblets, flasks, and their finest object, a glass bottle in the shape of a cluster of grapes.

The *Mosaic* section exhibits a dining room floor from a wealthy Roman villa that rested resplendent on the right bank of the river; the floor features Dionysus welcoming guests, swirling sea creatures, and the four seasons. Even more of interest, the eating benches were placed on four sides around the central motif, over undecorated geometric borders. (Why bother? They were covered up.) You can still see the burn marks from the lamps used next to each bench.

The *Economics* section displays *amphoras* for wine or olive oil. They were used only once, and to keep cool were often stuck in sand. Hence, perhaps, the pointed ends of those originating from the Mediterranean, though the point also made for another "handle" to make pouring easier. *Amphoras* originating in Gaul had fat tops and rounded bottoms.

Most surprising was a mockup of a huge, water-powered Roman grain mill, first discovered in the twentieth century. The mill once produced enough flour, almost 4.5 tons per day, to feed all 12,000 inhabitants of Arelate (Arles) in the fourth century AD. Its eight pairs of waterwheels turned volcanic millstones all day, every day, powered by water brought in via aqueducts through lead pipes. (You can see the pipes at the museum.)

You can visit the actual site of the **Barbegal mill**, twelve kilometers east of Arles, and climb along the length of the aqueduct to where the mill was installed, built in steps that made use of the natural drop of the hillside. *In situ*, the scope of the enterprise is astonishing. From the top you can still look out onto agricultural fields once irrigated by the mill runoff.

The view from the plunge of the Roman mill ruins at Barbegal.

Taberna Romana, Glanum

The Roman Emperor Tiberius had a famous chef working for him, Gavius Apicius, the most famous Roman gastronome we know of. The **Taberna Romana Restaurant**, run by Mireille Cherubini, attempts to recreate some of his recipes at their site right in the ruins of the Roman town known as Glanum, near Saint Rémy de Provence. Typical Roman ingredients go into *samsa*, a spiced olive paste, *cicerona*, a chickpea paste with cumin and garlic, *pinea*, a pine nut sauce with spices, and *phoenix*, a date and onion sauce. *Feniculum* is fennel prepared with honey and spices. You can try these at the restaurant and also take them home from the Taberna's shop.

Mouriès and the Olive Trail

This village is France's premier oil-producing municipality, with 80,000 olive trees and four different AOC olive oils. From November to December, harvest time, you can visit the town's three olive mills and stroll the **Alpilles olive trail**. The town honors its olive heritage with three festivals—one in August for *aioli* lovers, the **Green Olive Festival** the third week in September, and the **First Oil Festival** in early December. In nearby St. Rémy you can walk the grounds of the twelfth-century monastery of **St. Paul de Mausole**,

where in 1889 Vincent Van Gogh painted some of the expressive olive trees he observed while a patient at the asylum there.

Musée Camarguais

Housed in an old stable, this exhibition about the geology and geography of this unusual area also takes a look at how people lived and worked on the farms, or *mas*, here in the nineteenth century.

27

Musée du Riz en Camargue, Le Sambuc

At the end of a bouncy road, surrounded by rice fields, sits a small museum about the history of rice growing in the marshy lands of the Camargue. It's a region reminiscent of the Netherlands, with high banked fields and flatlands filled with heron and egret. The museum has seen better days, clearly—its passionate guiding light is still Robert Bon, rice king in these parts and the keeper of rice lore and legend. But, as he points out, literally—"that factory over there is closed"—there is simply no cultural tradition to support French rice growers, so their numbers are dwindling. He notes that there is no French tradition of preparing rice: "we do a version of *paella*, but it really is from Spain, we eat *risotto*, but we buy Italian rice in order to make it, Indian food too is prepared in France, but with rice from India."

And yet, for a true foodie, the museum is worth the trip—there is an old movie poster for *Riz Amer* with Vittorio Gassman and Sylvana Mangano, sickles and assorted hoes typical of French rice cultivation, a large sculpture of a grain of rice, as well as rice items for sale. In season, especially if you can meet Robert Bon, add this to your viewing of bulls, white horses, flamingoes, and other Camarguais offerings. (*Riz Amer* or Bitter Rice was a post-war thriller set in the Italian Po valley rice fields, with Ms. Mangano, up to her thighs in the watery rice field, winner of the first filmed wet t-shirt contest and fetching in then-shocking shorts.)

The annual three-week **Arles Rice Festival** or **Prémices du Riz**, held during the month of September, features horses, bull fights, marching bands, and parades, and acres of street-vendored *paella*, much of it dangerously *en pleine air* and reheated throughout the day. The people of Salin de Giraud, a salt production area for generations, host the final event of the Festival, cooking up a town-sized *paella* in a pan so large it takes four to carry it.

Not a contradiction in terms, France's paella *is a respectable cousin to that of Spain. It all starts with the pan—a flat, round pan, suitable for placing over fires heated to embers from stray wood.* Paella *itself means pan as does the French word* poêle, *the similarity confirming the shared origin of the word. The Romans brought the pan, the Arabs the rice, and the natives of the mouth of the Rhône River provided the seafood that predominates in French* paella.

Stage 7: Martigues to Carry le Rouet to Rove

Sampling the ancient specialties here involves munching slices of *poutargue* and blackened sardines on thick bread with tomatoes and olive oil, slurping down spoonfuls of sea urchin reproductive organs, and, for dessert, eating honey added to the wet, white cheese of the goats of Rove, among the lucky goats blessed with a view of the Mediterranean.

Poutargue, sometimes also called *boutargue*, was selling for 100 Euro per kilo just footsteps from the port in Martigues at **Neptune Coquillages** 3, quai Kléber. The owner gave us tastings of this mullet's egg delicacy, also known as caviar de Martigues, a treat that dates back here to at least the twelfth century. And probably even farther back to when the Greeks sailed to this port. *Poutargue* consists of egg casings that are salted, rinsed, flattened, and then dried in the air, and often covered with wax in order to preserve it for more than a week or two. (This manner of preparation was first mentioned in print in 1782.) It's eaten thinly sliced on buttered bread or bread dipped in olive oil.

You can also taste sea urchin here—the proprietor cut open a fresh urchin with a scissor-like tool developed years ago just for this purpose, scraped out its reproductive organs, and those we ate were very salty, very much direct from the sea.

Martigues celebrates all its seafood bounty on summer weekend evenings in typical *"sardinades"* where people grill and eat sardines along the banks of the canal.

Carry le Rouet

December to February visit the *oursinades*, sea urchin tasting events that comprise a festival.

29

La Ferme du Rove, Rove

Only 3,000–4,000 of these unusual Rove sheep live in France, their lyre-shaped horns their most distinctive feature. Ande Gouiran and his family may be the last Rove cheese producers in the small town of Rove itself. The sheep have lived here, with no unseemly genetic modifications, since the days when Greeks planted olive trees and vines in these hills, not far from their big city of Massilia, today's Marseilles, built about 600 BC.

The fifteen-generation Gouiran business involves two Border collies, Donna and Poupette, and about 280 goats. Their most delectable product may well be the *brousse de Rove*, fresh cheese made from whole milk, cut with vinegar, placed in paper cornets, and eaten either with fruit and sugar as a dessert or salted with bread as a snack.

Don't miss the goat statue in front of the town hall on your way to visit the farm. And try the bread down the hill at **Fournil de Rove**, an artisanal bakery where you can watch the bakers run through their bag of tricks.

Stage 8: Solliès-Pont to Collobrières to Le Rayol to Grimaud

Figs that melt in the mouth almost as gracefully as does the distinctive chestnut ice cream here. In this corner of Provence you can dine well in three differing environments—on the farm with your host and hostess, sampling organically raised pork and goat, at a hustle bustle crowded local watering hole, or in full formal linen country splendor in front of the fire, where braised *petits lapins* feature on the menu.

Solliès-Pont

Alas, Spain, Italy, Turkey, and Greece now supply most of France's appetite for figs, according to a local grower who said her grandparents once sold hundreds of baskets of figs in Paris each season. Still, the town of Solliès-Pont does its best to keep French figs in the picture. The variety "Violette de Solliès," a true local development, is aiming for an AOC label. You can drive past fig orchards here, buy some local fig products, and observe the unusual beauty of the twisty fig silhouette itself.

31

Collobrières

This pleasant village with a twelfth-century stone bridge and streets lined with buttonwoods is also a major chestnut center, still trying to maintain the traditions of the past even though the harvest is not what it used to be. Tourism handouts state that Collobrières has 2,200 acres of chestnut groves producing two hundred tons of chestnuts per year, yet some whisper that the chestnuts used in their annual festival actually come from China. Indeed, statistics reveal that France imports two-thirds of the chestnuts it consumes.

The town supports a chestnut confectionery business, the **Confiserie Azuréenne**, that not only turns chestnuts into *marrons glacés* (chestnuts glazed in sugar) and choco-late-covered delights, but also makes delectable chestnut ice cream. The town offers visitors a museum tour that explains how chestnuts are turned into sweets. (Rumors abound that even the *marrons glacés* arrive from Italy.)

One of the prime movers in establishing the festival is Loic de Saleneuve. "There are many chestnut trees still, but few interested in harvesting them anymore, alas," he says.

Loic and his wife Andrée own an organic farm and *table d'hôte* called **La Bastide de La Cabrière**, in a narrow valley outside of town. "We are peasants here at heart," says Loic, a Count who leaves his title way behind, "with a deep respect for this ancient land and its traditions." Known for their fine strawberries at the market in St. Tropez, the de Saleneueves' primary focus is goats, their own flock, and the cheese-making business the goats make possible. The young goats leap up from their pens, looking healthy and happy. Loic treats them homeopathically when needed and Andrée gives them daily tender care. You can book in as a guest here, sharing the table with your hosts, and sampling Loic's array of homemade *apéritifs* and yes, in season, eating goat. "The young males taste like lambs," they say. "Very delicious."

Restaurant Maurin des Maures, Rayol de Canadel

Dédé Del Monte's chef's whites are white jeans and a crisp, clean white shirt, symbolic of the warm and informal atmosphere at his restaurant, **Maurin des Maures**, named after a Provençal novel of the early 1900s. (The creation of Jean Aicard, the *maurin* is a Robin Hood-type mountain man, a rugged independent hero.)

Dédé's Italian last name comes from his grandfather—"around here everyone is a little bit Italian"—but his outlook is all Provençal all the time, albeit with the Var variation. His patrons are wealthy foreigners with summer homes, sitting cheek to jowl with the local constabulary and rugby enthusiasts. The tables sit a knife blade apart in tidy rows, so it's almost impossible not to relate to your neighbors. His photo wall of fame features a well-fed smiling Pierre Salinger, President John F. Kennedy's press secretary, "the most French American I ever knew," as well as English actress Charlotte Rampling.

As he darts in and out, serving up small plates of entrees with his secret "red sauce," he talks of the dangers of global warming, the huge merits of the Slow Food Movement, the need to educate young people about French food traditions, but also the return to organic products. His brother, a dessert chef, works with him, and we try his basil grapefruit ice cream, a treat so surprising and tasty that we laugh out loud.

Dédé will answer all your Provençal food history questions as he serves up "real" *bouillabaise*, presented on a large slab of cork—"these touristy restaurants will serve the same food, not as good, of course, on a silver platter and charge you for the platter," he says, laughing. His first book, *La Cuisine Complice*, has been published by Editions Aubanel.

Red Sauce, Sauce Roseline

Roseline's sauce, created by Dédé's mother, is a marvel. Though intended to accompany meats, this sauce is tasty on vegetables, as well as bread, and it would probably not go amiss served atop one of the vegetable sorbets served at the restaurant.

4 oily anchovy fillets
4 T. tomato concentrate
4 T. chopped parsley or fresh basil
4 chopped garlic cloves
4 T. olive oil
4 T. mustard
pepper mill

Crush the anchovy fillets, add the tomato concentrate, the parsley, the crushed garlic, the olive oil, and the mustard. Then add 4 turns of the pepper mill and mix together all ingredients.

Recipe courtesy Roseline and Dédé Del Monte, Restaurant Maurin des Maures, Le Rayol, Var, Provence. Editions Aubanel, France.

Hôtel Restaurant Coteau Fleuri, Grimaud

Tapenade in a pastry crust, baby rabbit in a creamy wine sauce, Irish lamb (!), oysters with Jerusalem artichokes, chopped vegetables in a broth, slivers of potato pastry filled with langoustines, Brittany scallops with fennel, celery and tarragon sauce, goat's cheese with truffles... At the **Hôtel Restaurant Coteau Fleuri**, in winter you dine in a cozy room facing a snapping fire. In summer, you sit overlook-ing a soft Provençal landscape, tangerine roses on the table. About seventeen years ago the owner host, Jacques Minard, bought the building, a former silk bobbin factory. His mission is to present the best wild and domesticated ingredients from all over France.

It's a hotel and an inn abutting a fifteenth-century chapel, a latecomer as the chateau dates back to the eleventh century.

Stage 9: Draguignan to Callas

Without the birds and the bees, but especially the bees, yes, we would have no food. And without the labors of the Provençal donkeys, there might have been no bees, and no olive oil. Provençal honey, as provided by the Jean-Philippe Mandard honey business, combines the old with the new, as does the family olive mill run by the Beringuiers. A look back at the hard life of both families' ancestors is magnificently captured in a little-known gem of an everyday arts museum in Draguignan.

Musée des Arts et Traditions Populaires, Draguignan

The terraced agriculture of the Var in Provence made the most of the stone-filled available ground. Using the stone, farmers built dry walls that enclosed their traditional plots. Rows of grape vines alternated with areas of grain, with olive trees and fruit trees interspersed. Beehives usually lined the edges of the fields and were moved seasonally.

Draguignan's imaginative museum is the best of its type, a fine introduction to the basics of Provençal country life, with vignette-style theatrical exhibits that draw the viewer into the scene. Many of today's foodies would trade their souls for the traditional Provençal kitchen set-up on display here—a red-tiled countertop taller than the norm that is at once a work station and cook top, fired underneath by coal, the perfect slow heat for luscious stews and layered desserts.

Other exhibits put the visitor right into assorted nineteenth-century scenes of olive milling (there were seven hundred olive mills in this one region alone), sheep herding, bee keeping, and the cork industry.

Apiculture Mandard, Draguignan

Three donkeys live on the grounds of this honey operation, a reminder of their centuries-old roles, moving hives from field to field in order to produce a range of fine honeys—acacia, lavender, rosemary, chestnut, and many more. These days the Mandards move 450–500 hives around all summer long, on flatbed trucks. Each hive produces about 120 kilos of honey per year. Take a tour of the honey operation, and be sure to sample their honeys as well as their meads.

Moulin de Callas, Callas

In Africa workers harvest olives with fake claws on their fingers, according to olive expert Serge Beringuier. Here in the Var this traditional enterprise uses little rakes or *peignes*, once made from wood, but now usually plastic, to gently zip the olives from the branches. Serge restored the old water-powered olive mill here, and has pushed hard to revitalize the regional olive oil industry, regularly producing award-winning olive oils. He wastes nothing from his trees, even burning olive waste or *"grignon"* in an Italian furnace to heat his home. You can buy olive wood artifacts as well as oils at this fourth-generation family place of business. **35**

Stage 10: Villeneuve-Loubet to Cagnes sur Mer to Nice

The man who reinvigorated French cuisine and suggested many ways to streamline its commercial production, Escoffier receives his tribute at a museum in his hometown of Villeneuve-Loubet. (If you have time, the **Olive** **Museum** in Cagnes has a few surprises.) The more downhome basics of Mediterranean French cooking, such as *socca*, turn up in Nice.

Musée Escoffier de l'Art Culinaire, Villeneuve-Loubet

Few foodies will be able to resist a visit to the childhood home of Auguste Escoffier (1846–1935), "the king of cooks, the cook of kings." Perhaps best known for its impressive collection of old menus, many displayed on the top floor,

at heart the museum is an homage to M. Escoffier, preserving his favorite knife and saucepan, his medals and honors, as well as one of his *toques*, or starched, white chef's hats. Pilgrims can even sit comfortably on a cozy loveseat, the better to stare across at an enormous painting of the Master.

Credited with creating the integrated "assembly line" modern restaurant kitchen, and simplifying and streamlining traditional multi-course restaurant meals, Master Escoffier headed the kitchens of the Savoy and Ritz-Carlton in London, and revitalized the Ritz in Paris. He also came up with sensible inventions such as a bread crumb machine and dehydrated potatoes for purée. He wrote cookbooks, worked to feed the hungry, and claimed his success largely derived from his female clientele and the dishes he created for them: *Pêche (Nellie) Melba* (a huge blowup of Nellie's autographed photo is on display), *Fraises Sarah Bernhardt*, *Poires Mary Garden*.

His museum on the town's main street, now named for him, is a light-filled, well-funded, inviting place. Just off the small entryway sits the original hearth with its eighteenth-century *tournebroche*, or rotisserie. Dogs, presumably just fed, were once enlisted to walk treadmill fashion in order to turn this type of spit. Young boys replaced the dogs, and one of them probably grew up to invent a counterweight system displayed here that liberated kitchen slaves from this task.

A red-tiled Provençal kitchen introduces the subject of stoves, its high counter cook top fired by charcoal burning below. This replaced the open hearth and began the trend towards more precise cooking. Several antique stoves illustrate the progress in cookery, including the 1850 gas cooker of another famous French chef, Alexis Soyer.

The museum contains an extensive library to be greatly expanded by 2005; it is finishing a new exhibition on the history of chefs, old and new, and will open a larger video-viewing visitor center as well.

Least appetizing item? A pastry train locomotive created in 1920.

Musée Ethnographique de l'Olivier, Cagnes

Stuck inside five rooms of the sprawling fourteenth-century Grimaldi Castle in Cagnes, the **Museum of the Olive Tree**, though looking a bit ragged and past its prime, still manages to convey solid information about olive milling. It particularly points out the hard labor of the little gray donkeys that worked the *moulins à sang* or blood mills of Provence before the harnessing of waterwheels. Items of interest: olivewood boxes and lap desks, a Roman granite mill base, and excellent clear explanatory drawings, sadly damaged by insects or worms.

A bonus: if you stray into the castle itself, you may be delighted to see, as we were, a central rain cistern, carefully protected, its water kept just for drinking. Evidently every "home" had one.

37

Restaurant Escalinada, Nice

In this town of exotic Phoenician delicacies like a *gnocchi* called "merda de can," or dog poop—delicious!—and a pancake made from chickpeas called "socca" —superb—you will not be eating *croque Monsieur*. You might not like the rotting-food, smelly-gym-socks odor, but the taste of *morues la maison* (smoked cod or stockfish, pounded and seasoned, pounded and seasoned) isn't bad. If not, there's always breaded sheep testicles on the menu.

This market street restaurant has a stamp of approval indicating that it serves genuine Nice specialties.

Socca, made from chickpea flour, is prepared on a large round copper pan and cooked in a hot wood-fired oven for about six minutes, until the top is golden. The heat spreads evenly in copper. *Socca* is a terrific portable food, served up with black pepper, full of protein and good taste, easily purchased at Nice's market. (Some *socca* makers deliver their tasty product to the market on the backs of specially designed bikes.)

Another moveable snack is the *pissaldiere*, the Nice pizza made with onions, olives, and anchovies.

Gnocchi verts or "merda de can"

Yes, it resembles what the family hound deposits. No, it tastes delicious. It's *gnocchi* in France. The deep dark color is provided by the well-cooked green chard.

Serves 6

2 lbs roughly chopped green chard
6 pounds floury potatoes
3 $^3/_4$ c. flour
2 eggs
Olive oil, salt, and pepper

Peel potatoes and bring to a boil in salted water. Blanch the greens in salted water for 5 minutes and drain well. Cut them as finely as possible, and place them back in a sieve. Squeeze any remaining water out of the chard. Drain the cooked potatoes through a ricer until finely "puréed," then place on a large bread board. Lightly beat the eggs and work well into the cooled potato, along with the greens, the flour, salt and pepper, and 1–2 tablespoons of oil. Once ingredients are well mixed together, knead gently 1 or 2 times, and let the mix sit for about 30 minutes. Roll out dough with a rolling pin or spread out the pasta with your hands. Cut into two-inch-long pieces, about $^1/_2$ inch across, and roll each between your palms. Drop into salted boiling water but cook at a low boil. When the pieces pop to the surface, remove them with a slotted spoon. Drain and serve either with a tomato sauce and cheese topping, or by drizzling olive oil on top, then cheese.

Adapted from a traditional recipe provided by Nice Office of Tourism.

Stage 11: Menton to Peille to Tourette to Pont du Loup

Two food festivals, the huge *Fête du Citron* in Menton, and its Medieval "survivor soup" event, underscore how and why food matters. A master lemon grower at *La Citronneraie* is helping to keep this Mediterranean food tradition prospering.

Fragrant herbs, flowers, and fruits are rooted in the hillsides of Provence.

We visit the ancient village of Peille, where tourism has not quite eclipsed its agricultural heritage, as well as a thriving, multifaceted violet establishment in Tourette, and a candy business carved out of a gorge under the Pont du Loup bridge once blown up by retreating Nazis.

Fête du Citron, Menton

Lemons, ah lemons, and the *tartes aux citrons*, a local divine specialty—the **Menton Lemon Festival** celebrated each February goes back 72 years (the Brazilian babes in the parade may not), but the lemon itself has been here far longer.

La Citronneraie, Menton

François Mazet, a lemon grower and citrus expert, says the lemon has grown in Menton for about three hundred years. The Arabs brought it to Spain much earlier, in the eighth century, though Mazet thinks the lemon hopped directly across the Mediterranean to Menton from Egypt.

Years ago 100,000 lemon trees grew in this region, but disease and frost killed off many groves. Today there are about 3,000 trees in Menton, and 250 trees of "Menton lemons" grow at La Citronneraie.

It takes twelve months to grow a lemon, plus fifty gallons of water per week, and copious amounts of horse manure, as well as loads of hand labor. Far quicker, says Mazet, than getting fruit from olive trees. He has some trees on his property that are five hundred to six hundred years old.

During the lemon festival you can visit daily, otherwise call ahead.

There's another food festival in Menton, one not entwined with Disney characters and massive citrus floats—

it's the **Fête des Bazais**, celebrated each year in August. It dates back to the Middle Ages when much of the population was wiped out by plague. The survivors were attacked by Barbary pirates, who destroyed or carried away their food stocks. Two plucky souls set out to find food and finally returned with weevil-infested black beans, for which they paid a fortune. Faced with famine, the people delighted in the beans, pooled their resources and made a large cauldron of soup, adding scraps of meat and varied bits of vegetables. This survival soup convinced the pirates they could never conquer the locals. Rather than recreate the weevily black bean soup, today the locals are inclined to make that garlicky Côte d'Azur favorite, *soupe au pistou*, more often than not.

Soupe au pistou

Pistou, of course, is the French version of *pesto*, and is similar except that the French do not include pine nuts in their mix. Plopped into a bowl of this exuberant vegetable soup, the *pistou* spreads its basil and olive oil across the surface.

1 ham hock

1 piece of pork rind (optional)
12 c. water
$^3/_4$ c. fresh green beans
4 potatoes of medium size
3 zucchinis

For the pistou
5 cloves of garlic
approx. 40 basil leaves
2 tomatoes

Note: Soak dried beans overnight.
1 c. dried white beans
$^3/_4$ c. dried kidney beans
3 tomatoes
$^1/_2$ c. spaghetti cut into pieces

olive oil
black pepper
2 oz. grated Edam cheese

Put the hock and the rind in a large stew pan. Cover with salted cold water. Boil the hock and the rind, then skim off the fat. Boil them for $1^1/_2$ hours.

Wash the beans. Peel and wash the potatoes and the zucchinis. Dip the tomatoes into boiling water for about 30 seconds. Remove the seeds and roughly mash them while removing the skin. Add all the beans, potatoes, whole zucchinis, tomatoes, and the pasta to the stewpan. Keep cooking on low fire for about 1 hour, stirring when necessary. Set aside.

Prepare the pistou
Peel the cloves of garlic. Wash the basil. Drain basil leaves on absorbent towels. Peel the tomatoes, remove the seeds, then chop them finely. Mash the basil and the garlic in a mortar, add salt. Add the chopped tomatoes, grated cheese, olive oil, and pepper. The mixture must be thick. Put this preparation in a soup bowl and set it aside.

Cook the zucchinis and the potatoes, remove them from the pan, and mash them with a fork. Remove the hock and cut it into small cubes. Put back all the ingredients into the soup kettle, mix together, and correct the seasoning if necessary. Stir in about two tablespoons of *pistou*.

Serve hot in large bowls, and let your guests add as much *pistou* as they wish.

Recipe courtesy Menton Tourism and www.cote.azur.fr.

The other fish soup of the southeast, soupe de poisson *is a thick fish broth traditionally ladeled over* rouille-*slathered toasted bread and topped with grated cheese.*

Musée du Terroir du Peille

At this small charming museum about everyday life, in one of France's prettiest perched towns, the artifacts and objects are labeled in the Peille dialect, one of the ancient Langue d'Oc languages before French. One item, the "mixing trunk" of the local priest, always held herbs he gathered and blended for infusions, *herbs de Provence* gathered in the wild.

Our guide, Jean-Paul Barelli, leading us there through the narrow streets with his bright-as-a-button cocker spaniel sidekick, told us that the women of the village would bring bread to the town baker, the loaves marked with a distinct pattern of apricots. Each family gave the baker a loaf in payment, and as this made a surplus, the bakery tradition began. The people were poor, repairing garments worn by more than one generation, and "recycling" their huge clay jars—for fifty to one hundred years they held olives or olive oil. Once they became a bit grungy, they were turned into latrines. Donkeys then pulled the filled pots out to the fields where the waste was used as fertilizer, much as many small-holding Chinese farmers still do today. The economic decline of Peille began with its loss

of fifty-two young men in World War I, a huge toll on one small village. "That was the beginning of the end of agriculture here," said Barelli. In 1972 Barelli started a local **Fête de Blé**, or wheat festival here that is held the first Sunday in August.

Les Violettes d'Yvette, Tourrettes-sur-Loup

Driving up to find the violet farm, the stone-terraced landscape is a mixed bag of old palms, cactus, and tall skinny cedars, all looking out to the turquoise Mediterranean. This is the only place in France where violet cultivation is the primary agricultural endeavor. (Louis XIV liked violet blossoms strewn in his salads.) Yvette Boselli-Osteng, a vivacious former accountant, has been running

her violet business here for over twenty years. As with many such ventures, thirty years ago there were sixty violet growers. Today, there are about six. You'll recognize her place in winter by the rows of fava beans growing near the entrance.

Violets, lovers of cool nights, low humidity, and ample sun, bring profit in three ways. First, their October to March bloom is cut for bouquets, each containing twenty-five flowers. Yvette sells about 25,000 of these each winter. From January to March, their larger blooms are harvested for use in candy making. Then, in May and in August the leaves are gathered for their aromatic extracts and sent to Grasse perfume companies.

You can visit Yvette's place by dropping in or by making an appointment for groups in advance by phone.

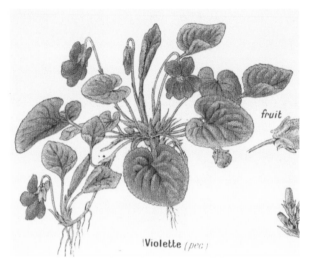

Violette *(pec)*

Confiserie Florian, Pont du Loup

You can taste Yvette's violets here, all candied up—Florian's processes four hundred kilos of violets each year. But you can also dip into lemon and orange strips enveloped by chocolate, glazed clementines with all the juice tucked inside, bonbons containing ten Provençal flavors or aromas, as well as rose petal jam and jasmine jam. One gentleman we met proposed a new "floral" drink—first a dollop of violet jam, then champagne.

Take a tour, taste at will, and then walk through the terraced garden designed and developed by Confiserie Florian's owner, Frédéric Fuchs, to showcase the plants that go into his confections—roses, citrus trees, jasmine, lavender, and herbs. One ton of roses and six tons of citrus whip through his candy maker's hands each year. A new idea? How about verbena leaves dipped in sugar...

The Confiserie has been in business since just after World War II, but the family's first enterprises were in perfume.

Stage 12: Les Bourelles to Manosque

Young braised pigeons and olive oil-soaked bread made up a typical meal of the Middle Ages, as the pigeon museum people of Les Bourelles will tell you.

It was Jany Glieze of **La Bonne Etape** who suggested we visit the *pigeonnier* in the first place. While Chef Glieze buys his pigeons from a nearby monastery, he recommends the **Ecomusée** to visitors who want to do more than just taste. His La Bonne Etape in Chateau Arnoux is a legendary hotel restaurant, an eighteenth-century *relais*, or coaching inn set in a small town surrounded by olive tree-lined lavender fields.

Food writer and cook Patricia Wells, an American who lives in Provence much of the year, wrote about La Bonne Etape's *tarte au citron et au chocolate* in her 1987 classic *Food Lover's Guide to France*. She described a delectable dessert created from a mistake, and suggested this was not to be missed. Alas, it is no longer on the menu, so after a superlative meal of asparagus with truffles, *coquilles* with wild mushrooms, pigeon breasts, and lamb, we accepted as a consolation prize a concoction involving lavender ice cream and a coppery spun sugar structure a millionaire spider might have enjoyed in her playground.

(Chef Glieze was amused by the fact that American and Japanese tourists were always showing up with that book in their hands, asking for dessert.)

In this part of ungussied-up Alpes de Haute Provence you can sample many of the food specialties from one of the sunniest of French regions, in village after village set up in the hills near the Durance River. Olive oils from the perched town of Lurs, lamb from Sisteron, cheese wrapped in chestnut leaves from Banon, liqueurs from the limestone-based village of Forcalquier—such delights make this region one of those flagged in its entirety as a *Site Remarquable du Goût*.

Just by chance, on the road to Mane, we came across a two-year-old cooperative store, the **Maison de Produits du Pays de Haute Provence**, selling regional specialties and artwork, as well as unusual books on a wide range of food and agriculture subjects published by Alpes de Lumiére.

Ecomusée des Pigeonniers de Haute-Provence at Le Moulin Fortune Arizzi, Les Bourelles

At the lovely old 1574 farm known as **Le Mas des Pins** you can visit a working 8,000-tree olive business and also view a small but fascinating exhibition about pigeons and pigeon houses, in a restored eighteenth-century *pigeonnier* on the property. Pigeons still come and go from the upper stories of the tower, protected from predators by a band of glazed tiles, very slippery to cat toenails. Never fed except in severe cold weather, the pigeons glean food from nearby fields.

Just below you can view assorted pigeon holes, different varieties of bird, and learn much about the architecture of French pigeon houses. The number of pigeon holes per house usually reflected the wealth of the farm owner.

Pigeons, particularly the young nestlings, were valued as a source of free food, as well as for their powerful fertilizer used in olive groves, vineyards, and kitchen gardens.

La Thomassine Biodiversity Center, Manosque

Over three hundred varieties of heirloom fruit trees are growing here, as well as a myriad of vegetables. The Center preserves seed and heirloom plants, offers lessons in gardening and sustainable agriculture, and welcomes visitors in season.

Stage 13: Bonnieux to Cavaillon to L'Isle sur Sorgues and Menerbes

Good bread, the melons that became the symbol of Cavaillon, and some country wine—if you visit the wine seller tucked off the bustling market area in Isle sur Sorgues, he'll provide just the right choice of each for your picnic. Try the tapenade and explore the food-related antiquities in this foreign visitor mecca.

Melons of Cavaillon

Honored by a gargantuan statue in town, the Cavaillon green-striped netted melon has been this area's most famous product since the mid-1800s, though it probably began growing here in the Middle Ages. Alexander Dumas loved these melons so much he donated three hundred of his books to the town in exchange for twelve melons a year, thereby founding the town's library. We did not venture into the library to see if his books are still there on the shelves, but we doubt very much that Dumas descendants still receive free melons. The melon festival takes place here the second week in July.

Le Musée de la Boulangerie, Bonnieux

A project of the local baker's union, this exhibition in a seventeenth-century building did once house a bakery, and its oven was used until the 1920s. Exhibits cover all things baking, including tools, methods, types of grain, as well as old engravings and advertising materials.

45

Isle sur Sorgues

Sorgues is the antiques center of the Luberon region made famous by the books of Peter Mayle. If you're a collector of old food-related items, be sure to walk the market. We bought two old linen-lined baguette baskets, supposedly used to cool the loaves at the edge of the oven.

Sorgues is also the home of **Les Délices du Luberon**, producers of olive specialties. Their tapenade, typical of the region, combines olives, capers, and anchovies. And their shop is a mini olive museum, with old advertising materials, containers, measuring cans, and an extensive olive pitter collection. A nineteenth-century gadget on a high shelf was used to measure the fluidity of olive oil.

You can taste away here.

Musée du Tire-Bouchon, Menerbes

The corkscrew may well be a seventeenth-century English invention, a variation on a device used to extract the charge from some kind of gun. But a French tale relates that a couple of vinous lads, accustomed to corking their bottles with just enough sticking out so as to extract the cork with one's teeth, became well sloshed one night. Discovering they had jammed the cork deep into the one remaining bottle, they grabbed a length of vine, attached it to a screw from their carriage and set about to extract the cork. The screw/vine combo worked, the lads were reunited with their wine, and thanks to a blacksmith friend, a cork removal device was created that has survived in its essence to this day. In any event, the oldest corkscrew in this 1,000-plus collection is a seventeenth-century French piece. Up until the nineteenth century corkscrews were highly individual, handcrafted items, often marked with the owner's initials. Visit the museum and tour the vineyards.

Stage 14: Nyons to Villeneuve de Berg to Montélimar

Immerse yourself in olives and almonds this trip, from this northern range of the olive tree in Nyons, just on the cusp of where people eat more butter than oil, to the old almond center of France in Montélimar. On the way, stop off at the home of one of the almond's promoters.

The olive is well honored in Nyons. The **Institut du Monde de l'Olivier**, an olive information center, is based here and does occasional olive exhibitions. The local olive growers' cooperative runs the **Musée de l'Olivier** where curator René Gras shows visitors the museum's fourth-century Roman olive oil lamps, pottery crocks, uniquely Nyons-style olive-picking ladders with one central rail, hand tools for plucking olives from the branches, and a couple of nineteenth-century olive oil presses. Nyons natives often traded their labor for oil. You can also see photos, at least, of 1,000-year-old area olive trees. In 1956 a huge freeze devastated olive trees all over France, though the curator was quick to point out that only the tops of the trees were killed (still, there was little production as the trees recovered). The La Tanche black olive tree is Nyons' own, first planted by the Romans. From it come black table olives, olives for Provençal tapenade, and olives for oil. Nyons was the first olive oil area to receive the AOC.

Also in Nyons is the remarkable **Les Vieux Moulins**, tucked against the medieval bridge. The main olive mill here ran from 1850 until 1952, but the owner, Jean-Pierre Autrand, knew his family had been in the oil business from the eighteenth century. He learned this one day when he began cleaning out the basement of the property; literally digging down in the soft earth, he discovered a twin find—the family's eighteenth-century olive oil mill

and next to it an eighteenth-century soap-making operation. Olive oil soap was always made from the final pressed dregs of oil, the same oil used in lamps. (He also found guns, presumably stashed by his Protestant family, hidden in the bridge's foundations, and "escape" tunnels leading to and from the olive mill.) You can see these underground finds and also his family's restored eighteenth-century apartment, plus wander the extensive olive-themed shop.

Down the road visit the place where the *escourtins* have been woven since 1880 at **La Scourtinerie**—*escourtins* are the rough pads used with mill wheels to extract oil from crushed olives. In the old days these were woven from straw. But when the mills began to use steel instead of wood, the straw pads didn't hold up—Ferdinand Fert decided to make new pads of water-resistant coconut fiber, imported from India. His innovation changed the business that continues at the weaving workshop to this day, only now most woven pads are being used as carpets, doormats, and bathmats—the big freeze effectively ended the factory's major business. The current owner and descendant of the founder still does custom weaving of pads for the new wave of artisanal olive operations.

His workshop is intriguing and the shop sells all sizes and colors of pads.

Overlooking Nyons' large town square, the comfortable **Hôtel Restaurant Colombet** has kept an eye on its citizens' comings and goings for generations. The restaurant's menu reflects the tasty olive-based traditions of the region. Try their simple, satisfying tapenade, slathered on bread or crackers or layered in cooked chicken fillets topped with cream.

47

Provençal tapenade

An olive spread familiar to the Romans, tapenade on crusty pieces of bread makes a meal.

Serves eight

2 lbs Nyons black olives (pitted)
$^{1}/_{8}$ c. garlic
$^{3}/_{4}$ c. capers
1 c. anchovies
8 $^{1}/_{2}$ T. Nyons olive oil

Pour the garlic, capers, and anchovies into a blender. Mix them together on low, adding a bit of olive oil. Then, add pitted olives, blending with more oil until you obtain a soft creamy consistency. Refrigerate until ready to serve.

Recipe courtesy Hôtel Restaurant Colombet.

Centre de ressources du Domaine Olivier de Serres, Mirabel

For Olivier de Serres (1539–1619), often described as the father of modern French agriculture, the ideal garden was divided into four parts—vegetables, flowers, medicinal herbs, and the orchard. Each was to be beautiful as well as productive. The Olivier de Serres exhibition reflects the same values. His home, **Le Pradel** at Mirabel, is at once an experimental farm, school, and museum. De Serres, a Protestant, lived at a time when, under the 1598 Edict of Nantes, French Protestants enjoyed official toleration, but in practice often lacked civil rights and were even persecuted; de Serres' home was burned to the ground by the King's army in 1608 and rebuilt two years later by his son.

You can walk the gardens and examine the exhibits. The person who introduced silk worms to France, de Serres also was an early chronicler of two native American foods, the tomato and the potato, writing one of the earliest and clearest descriptions of the tuber in his famous book published in 1600, *Théâtre d'Agriculture et Mesnage des Champs*. His book, with a title difficult to translate, covers what de Serres considered to be the "best practices" in agriculture. It went through nineteen printings until the revocation of the Edict of Nantes in 1685, then was forgotten until a new edition appeared once again in 1804. It still remains in print.

When de Serres was only two, the potato was brought to this region from Toledo, Spain, by an elderly Franciscan monk named Pierre Sornas, who was returning home to live out his remaining days with his family. Saint-Alban d'Ay, a village about fifty miles from de Serres' home, may be the spot where the potato was first planted in France. The locals called it *"truffole,"* after the truffle which early chroniclers thought it resembled. Many here still call *pommes de terre "truffoles"* today.

Blossoming almond trees from an early twentieth-century postcard.

Olivier de Serres's statue in Villeneuve de Berg.

Nougaterie Arnaud Soubeyran and Le Chaudron d'Or, Montélimar

If you like nougat, you can thank de Serres for promoting the growing of almonds in the region. Abundant almond trees eventually made nearby Montélimar the center of nougat production. The **Nougaterie Arnaud Soubeyran**, established in 1837, offers visitors a small museum called the **Nougathèque**, which covers this candy's history. **Le Chaudron d'Or**, a nougat manufacturer that has produced fifty tons of handmade nougat a year since 1949, mixes Provence lavender honey, egg whites, Spanish almonds, Sicilian pistachio nuts, and vanilla extract from La Réunion. Or at least it tries to use these traditional ingredients—American pistachios were more cost-effective for years.

You can tour the place every day of the week to learn the details of nougat history and production, and to taste to the point of a sugar high.

49

East:
Rhone, Bourgogne, and Franche-Comté

Sitting at a banquet table in the **Brasserie le Français** in Bourg-en-Bresse, our backs to the mirrored wall, our noses were picking up the subtle flavors of the house-marinated *saumon fumé* on a bed of wilted lettuce. When we tasted the frogs' legs aperitif, we were slightly surprised by the springy quality of the little shapely legs awash in parsley butter.

We sipped champagne and waited, without a dot of impatience, hands on the apricot linen tablecloth, for the restaurant's specialty chicken dish. The bird is roasted, then cut up and lightly warmed in full cream before being served with wild morel mushrooms. Rich but simple. (The *pommes Dauphinois* served with the chicken was equally voluptuously rich.)

We had met the fine-feathered, blue-footed AOC birds that morning, as pampered a flock as the black and white *foie gras* ducks of Frespech, on a farm run by Christophe Vouillol. Walking his fields with his young in-training Australian sheepdog, and then sitting in the Brasserie, we knew we were in the heart of traditional French cooking. A productive region, shielded on the east and west by mountains and rich with extensive wine growing, its fertile soils are supported by the Rhône river valley and its tributaries.

This is the France of good bread, cheese and mustard, potatoes, creamy sauces, Côte du Rhône, Beaujolais and Burgundy wines, eggs, chickens, frogs, and snails.

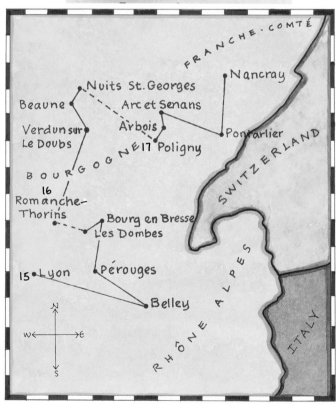

50

Poulet de Bresse au Champagne

Chicken as divine sustenance. Try it.

One 5-lb. top-quality chicken
4 shallots
$^2/_3$ c. butter
$^1/_2$ bottle Brut champagne
2 c. chicken broth
2 $^1/_2$ c. crème fraîche
salt and pepper

Cut chicken into 8 pieces and cook in 50 grams of butter in a large heavy skillet at fairly high heat, to seal in the flavor.

Remove chicken to a hot plate and place roughly chopped shallots in the pan, cooking them for about 5 minutes.

Place chicken back in the pan and add champagne.

Cook for about 10 minutes, then add the broth, mix well, and continue cooking for another 15 minutes.

Remove the chicken again, add the crème fraîche to the pan, bring juices to a boil, and reduce the sauce.

Remove from the fire, and add the remaining butter. Taste and add salt or pepper as needed.

Cover chicken with hot champagne sauce and serve at once.

Recipe created by Gerard Boyer, Reims, and made available courtesy Poulet Bresse, www.pouletbresse.com.

51

Stage 15: Lyon to Belley to Pérouges to Bourg en Bresse to Les Dombes

You can eat your way through Lyon, a UNESCO World Heritage Site, chosen for its 2,000 years of urban design, and then proceed to gaze at the home of the physiological food maestro, Brillat-Savarin. Sample *galettes*, as well as breasts, thighs, and legs from local chickens and imported frogs.

Lyon

Even the fabled Lyonnaise chef Paul Bocuse suggested to writers of the *Let's Go France* guidebook that average mortals can eat extremely well in his town's *brasseries*, though no one need avoid the higher echelon food meccas, of course. The entire city is known for its classic French culinary heritage and bounty of fine ingredients, many of which

Gruyère-rich Pommes Dauphinois at Brasserie Français

visitors can sample and buy at Lyon's spectacular huge market, **La Halle**, established in 1850. There are fifty-eight vendors here as well as several of Lyon's famous cafe-restaurants, *bouchons*, their food offerings originally created from everyday butchers' trimmings, offal, or animal viscera.

Brillat-Savarin birthplace, Belley

"Tell me what you eat and I will tell you what you are," wrote Jean Anthelme Brillat-Savarin (1755–1826.) A judge by profession, and later mayor of Belley, Brillat-Savarin was the author of the gastronomy classic *The Physiology of Taste*. His birthplace site welcomes visitors into the courtyard but not the house itself. Extolling the virtues of chocolate, and truffles, and of eating well, Brillat-Savarin wrote that "the pleasures of the table are for every man"—and woman, thank you. He may be most vividly known, however, for his ninety-nine-year-old sister Pierrette's last words—"Quickly! Bring me dessert—I think I may be about to die."

52

Pérouges

Founded by a band of Gauls returning from the Italian town of Perugia, Pérouges was on its last medieval legs in the early 1900s when it was rescued from destruction by the Beaux Arts commission. Since then it has thrived as an almost-intact medieval environment and tourist magnet now well-known for its caramelized sugar galette, a simple, tasty tart with a hint of lemon zest.

Families sold baked goods and other wares right from their homes, on ledges like this one, built under their ground-floor windows.

Bourg en Bresse

You can visit a chicken farm such as that of Christophe Vouillol and observe the pleasant, brief lives these well-fed birds lead. After three to four months of wandering and scratching up bugs in green fields under the watchful eye of a young Border collie, the birds are placed in cages for the final fattening up, fed exclusively on milk-soaked corn (maize). Check with the local Tourism Office for a farm visit.

Bugey

Bread has indeed been the common daily food of most people for generations in France, with perhaps some simple cakes tossed in.

Before there were *boulangeries*, feudal lords and the Church owned the ovens in which their serfs baked their daily breads. The baker kept the ovens going and, since the bread of every household was all in the heat together, gave each family's loaves a distinctive slash. True, bread does split open on its own, but the slashes insured both ownership and a nicer look. Oven control by lords and priests eventually was replaced by that of the community. In Bugey some ovens remain, used on holidays and to entertain tourists in the summer.

The notion that the French became known as Frogs because of their dining preferences appears to be false. The Dutch, dwellers in reclaimed moist polder land, were historically depicted in eighteenth-century political cartoons as frogs, with the French lampooned as baboons, a reference to the Bourbon kings. After the Revolution the eating of frogs was identified as an enslavement to superstitious Catholic Church rulings and as a form of sustenance of the poor, who had to snatch amphibians from ponds in order to survive.

Les Dombes and frogs

The Dombes has traditionally been a wet, fishy, amphibiously rich region. Back in the twelfth century, building from a naturally moist area, farmers created *étangs* or ponds in order to raise fish. Every three years each pond was drained and planted in grain, then put back into the water business after harvest. Over the years people began to catch frogs along the banks of the ponds and happily sauté them with garlic and butter.

And yet—at the 2004 30th annual frog festival in Vittel, the mineral water town, the six tons of frogs eaten there all came from Indonesia, nicely vacuum-packed.

Most people know that frogs are the canaries in the mineshaft of world environmental health, and their numbers began to drop in Europe and elsewhere for a variety of reasons, including habitat destruction, increased use of agricultural chemicals and sprays, global warming, and depletion of the ozone layer.

In the 1980s frogs from India and Bangladesh replaced local amphibians worldwide until those countries, beset with infestations of malaria-carrying mosquitoes (one frog eats about 150 mosquitoes a day), realized they needed their frogs at home, and banned exports. Today Indonesia supplies much of the world's appetite for frog legs, including that of the French.

A local woman told us that as a child she used to go frog hunting with her grandfather. They used a simple wood pole, and attached to it a clear line on which they tied a tiny piece of red cloth. (Apparently the two characteristics shared by bulls and frogs are their strong legs and their attraction to the color red.) Madame said the frogs would grab hold of the cloth firmly with their "tiny teeth" and thus be captured and swung into an ordinary fisherman's net.

She sniffed at the notion of eating "foreign frogs," and implied that few French people from the Dombes would ever do so. After our chat, we drove in the dark to the tiny village of St. André le Bouchou, said to be frog central, supposed home of *les grenouillards*. We photographed this local café restaurant sign.

Stage 16: Romaneche-Thorins to Verdun sur le Doubs to Beaune to Nuits St Georges

A loaf of bread, a jug of wine, and thou, as Omar Khayam put it. We add mustard, and cassis.

Le Hameau du Vin, Romaneche-Thorins

If you like razzmatazz and marketing showmanship, and have time for only one wine museum, try this wine village, an entertaining sales tool of the Georges du Boeuf wine operation. You can easily spend two hours here, what with the audiovisuals and lively Disney-style exhibits all about wine making, barrel and glass making, the culture of vines, and the history of the Beaujolais traditions, plus a café and a 1900s recreated rail station—as well as tastings, naturally. Evidently du Boeuf, the largest producer and seller of Beaujolais wine, was one of the first promoters of the Beaujolais Nouveau craze.

Maison du Blé et du Pain, Verdun sur le Doubs

Traditional good French bread dates back at least to the Gauls, inventors of the first grain harvesting "machine," made of wood and designed to be pushed, rather than pulled. In this museum you can see a model of the Gaulish creation and also an example of a *tribulum*, a Roman sled made of attached wood planks embedded with sharp flints. Animals dragged these over wheat in order to separate the berries from the chaff. The museum tells the story of both wheat and baking, with a side trip to corn (maize) thrown in. As the convoluted legend goes, some Spanish folks coming from Milan on their way to Holland brought corn from the Americas to the Bresse region in the early sixteenth century. The result? Corn-fed chickens, and a porridge called *gaude*, eaten hot or cold, and corn as the major grain eaten in Bresse up until World War I.

Not only does the visitor learn the European history of bread and baking here—if you show up at the right time students are baking bread in the museum's huge wood oven. Say thank you to the seventh-century St. Honoré, patron of bakers, almost always pictured with his peel, before you rip a piece of bread off the still-warm loaves.

Musée de la Vigne et du Vin, Beaune (Burgundy Wine Museum)

Winemaking tools and machines as well as the history of the region are on display in this former home of one of the Dukes of Burgundy.

La Moutarderie Fallot, Beaune

Call it mustard theater, in truth, for the mustard museum opened by the last independent mustard milling company in Beaune, **La Moutarderie Fallot,** is just that. You start the tour in the dark, and as the lights come up images play across the walls, and bits of mustard history flap by you. Mustard gave Queen Victoria a pleasant buzz, for example, and *verjus* or green juice, the unfermented juice from the crushing of unripe grapes, insured French mustard its distinct smooth taste (vinegar was considered too acidic). Center stage are the old grinding stones of Fallot Ets.

Rapidly you are seduced and primed for your journey into "the mystery of mustard," in your choice of Japanese, Italian, English, or German, if French does not suit. An amusing audiovisual animation in the next room spins the tale of a greedy priest attempting to extract the secret mustard recipe from a naive mustard seller. Even better—you, the visitor, can now try your hand at grinding your own mustard mix: four mortars and pestles are set up for the purpose, with vinegar, salt, and mustard grains at hand. Yes, most of the grains are imported from Canada, but Fallot is part of a growing movement to revive local growing of the plant and make Burgundy Mustard an IGP, a product carrying the label *Indication Géographique Protégée*.

Leaving behind your own hapless mustard preparation, you climb the stairs to the nineteenth-century mustard maker's loft, filled with noisy machinery (again, the *museographique* system) and impossibly, the odor of fresh crushed mustard grains (the museum designers have allowed the distinct fragrance of mustard production to waft in from Fallot's small modern mustard factory next door). Tastings do follow, with the rose-colored *Dijon cassis* mustard top of the line. Another favorite—*Dijon moutarde aux pain d'epices*— the spicy bread of the region comprises 1.6 percent of the ingredients, along with added fruit flavors.

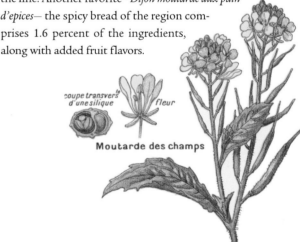

coupe transvers
d'une silique

fleur

Moutarde des champs

Queues de lotte à la moutarde et au basilica

Regional mustard adds the zip to this monkfish dish.

4 monkfish tails (you can also use turbot)
4 T. good quality French mustard
1 T. chopped shallots
1 T. chopped parsley
6 mushrooms
1 glass dry white wine
3 T. *crème fraîche*
1 sprig fresh parsley
salt and ground pepper

Clean and finely mince the mushrooms.

Heat the oven to 425 degrees F and place the mushrooms, chopped shallots, and parsley in a shallow ovenproof pan. Add the wine, spread the mustard on the fish, and place in the pan. Bake for 20 minutes.

Remove pan from oven, remove fish to a hot serving plate, and bring "juice" to a boil, adding the *crème fraîche* to make a sauce with a syrupy consistency. (You may need to whisk in a bit of corn starch.)

Salt and pepper to taste. Add to fish platter and top fish with a few basil leaves. Serve hot.

Recipe courtesy Maille Mustards. www.maille.com

Cassissium, Nuits St Georges

As you drive through the inviting villages of Burgundy country, you may well wonder what those shrubby-looking plants are, appearing in neat rows, sometimes alternating with the grape wines, in vineyard after vineyard. They are black currants, among the finest in the world, and many are transformed into the rich, purple *cassis* liqueur, in and around Nuits St Georges and Dijon. Currants and grapes thrive in the same soils and growing conditions of this region. In fact, at the close of the nineteenth century those local vintners who had planted black currants managed financially to survive the *phylloxera* infestation that wiped out the majority of their grape vines. Burgundians began mixing *cassis* liqueur and the famous white Burgundy Aligoté in the nineteenth century to create *Vin Blanc Cassis*, a drink today known more popularly around the world as Kir.

The Cassissium museum pops up above its own black currant hedge.

Most likely a native of Scandinavia, the currant was first cultivated in the early 1600s in Denmark and the Netherlands. The red currant became most popular for food, the black a favorite for jams, jellies, and, of course, liqueur.

From earliest times the black currant was prized as a medicinal herb, good for the vapors, and as an antidote for insect, scorpion, and snake bites, and its leaves worked wonders on migraines when draped across the sufferer's aching head. But by the mid-1700s the French were more enamored of its alcoholic properties—one of the earliest recipes for *cassis* liqueur came from the Abbé Bailly de Montaran, who mixed black currants with sugar and *eau-de-vie*, a formula that seems to be standard to this day. (The English evidently raise even more black currants than the French, but they daub them on toast and scones rather than drink them.)

A local manufacturer of *cassis* products, Védrenne, established in 1923, recently created a gem of a museum devoted to the history of the black currant. Cassissium features detailed colorful displays about the historical black currant and its use in medicine, the perfume business (remember "Chamade" by Guerlain?—it was the first black currant bud-based *couture* perfume), and in food and liquor products. It includes dozens of artifacts in a well-lighted exhibition space, and all the labeling is in French. To fill in any linguistic gaps you can request to see the exhibition's introductory film in French, German, English, or Japanese. The film is lively enough for children to enjoy, though its rotund bouncy hero, Supercassis, may begin to grate on adult viewers.

Right next to the museum is a production unit of the Védrenne firm where visitors can take a guided tour and see Supercassis Védrenne being made.

As if the voluptuous offerings of wines are not enough in Burgundy country, at Cassissium you can sample a remarkable range of *cassis* concoctions, including non-alcoholic drinks for kids. A young, gracious staff subtly yet generously ensures that you are drawn into the museum's well-stocked shop in a buying mood. Beware: the top-of-the-line version of *Supercassis Védrenne* is twenty-five percent proof and goes down like velvet.

Escargotière des Sources, Pouilly en Bassigny

Those quintessentially French critters, *les escargots* or snails, along with frogs and turtles, long ago were designated as "fish" by the Catholic Church and thus given the benediction for consumption on Holy Days. Even so, snails have been in and out of favor culinarily in France, according to historians, with their nadir being the three hundred years between the sixteenth and the nineteenth centuries.

Much as we may enjoy chomping down the garlic butter-and parsley-imbued snail, and dipping good bread into the residue, were we compelled to bring the snail from harvest to the table ourselves, most of us would have long since turned to a simpler form of protein. Plump snails ready for harvest must first evacuate their bodies of all food. Yes, they eat nothing for about fifteen days. Then they are boiled very briefly to kill them and allow their removal from the shells.

Intestinal bits that people do not eat are eliminated as well. Then they are soaked in salt so that their slime can exit, they are blanched in vinegar, salt, and water to remove any salmonella or bacteria, and finally, they are gently cooked up in a *court-bouillon* or water with wine  before being canned. If you have ever encountered a tough-to-chew snail basking in butter, now you know why.

Valérie Samec trained as a viticulturist but could find no work in that field. She turned to snails nine years ago, made a success of it, and now her home in Pouilly en Bassigny is easily identified as the one with the huge wood-carved snail out front. (Her husband built a sterilized hospital-white "lab" for her snail operation.)

Her 100,000 snails live outside from May until their demise in October, staying up all night to munch on barley. Throughout the season she welcomes visitors for snail tours and tastings. If you call in advance she'll prepare *escargots à la crème*, but this is not to be construed as a meal, just a tasting, otherwise it's not legal.

Stage 17: Poligny to Arbois to Arc et Senans to Pontarlier to Nancray

Discover this region's yellow cheese and wine, and visit the home of the man some call the father of modern winemaking. Gaze at UNESCO's saltiest World Heritage Site, and recall that absinthe made some hearts grow exceedingly wild.

Snow still lingered on the steep rooftops in the village of Arbois, close to the Jura Mountains, and we smelled wood smoke in the air as we parked in front of the tourism office. Both combined to whip up an appetite for the melted cheese dishes, including fondue, and the creamy wild mushroom dishes the area is known for. All dishes are enjoyed locally with the fine but less well-known Jura wines. Two in particular, the *Vin Jaune* and *Vin de Paille*, are found nowhere else.

Maison du Comté, Poligny

The Jurassic period, when dinosaurs rumbled the earth nibbling on cycads, is actually named after the rock formations of the Jura Mountains, "folded" rock that forms the border with Switzerland. This region of harsh winters and moist summers is home to contented Montbéliard cows and their splendid AOC Comté cheese (more Comté is produced than any other AOC cheese). Clearly here you understand why people first converted milk into preservable food. This is a cheese born to be lightly melted, and eaten with small perfect potatoes—wait, that's a Swiss dish—creation of the people and bovines of the Jura Massif.

Comté is not one of those cheeses that always tastes the same, even though strict quality standards govern its production. We learned this and more at the extremely handsome Comté cheese headquarters, where you can explore cheese-making without putting on the booties, white coats,

and hairnets we wore for an actual tour of a cheese-making operation (nor do you have to inhale the moist, "cowish," not altogether delectable aromas of the cheese biz, what the cheese-making intern described further as "somewhat suffocating").

Watch a video, examine large copper kettles and cheese rounds, even catch up on the history of Comté TV ads, and then taste every variety of Comté cheese available.

And then, if you want more, arrange with the Comté people to visit a cheese-making operation early in the morning. (We visited the **Arbois Cooperative Fromagerie**.)

White-garbed men in white boots stand on wet cement floors, poised over swirling white pools of milk in the main room, while others tap and probe and turn and wash the huge rounds of Comté patiently perched on shelves in the cave. Afterwards? More tasting and an opportunity to buy Comté direct from the Fromagerie.

Comté Cheese Fritata

A puffy omelet makes an ideal showcase for France's most popular cheese.

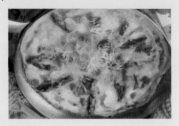

Serves 4

1 medium onion, sliced
olive oil
8 eggs
1 c. milk
6 steamed and chopped sun-dried tomatoes
salt, cayenne, and nutmeg to taste
6 oz. jambon français (ham), cubed
1 1/2 c. packed grated Comté cheese
8 asparagus steamed until tender

Preheat oven to 400 degrees. Sauté sliced onion in olive oil until soft. Set aside.
Beat eggs with the milk and add tomatoes, onions, and seasonings. Mix together, and add the cheese and ham.

Heat olive oil in heavy skillet, pour egg mixture in, and cook over medium heat for a few minutes. Arrange asparagus on top. Place skillet in the oven and cook until puffed up, about 10–20 minutes.

Recipe courtesy Comté Cheese Association.

Musée de la Vigne et du Vin, Arbois

When we arrived in this capital of Jura wine country, a viticulturist was trimming the grape vines growing in front of the restored medieval **Château Pecauld**, one tower of which once was part of the town's ancient walls.

Arbois' wines were the first in France to carry the AOC label, and the region's vineyards are among France's oldest, with a history spanning almost 5,000 years. (Both the Roman Pliny the Younger and Belgian songwriter and performer Jacques Brel evidently were big fans of Jura wines.) Inside you meet an eighteenth-century wine press, corking machines, and old bottles, as well as the photos, paintings, and stories of the wine producers themselves. Each September the village celebrates the ancient **Fête du Biou**, when the first pick of the harvest is carried through the streets and then blessed in the church. The *Vin Jaune*, a bright yellow wine with a hint of walnuts, along with its sweet dessert wine, *Vin de Paille* (in which three varieties of grapes dry completely on straw bales before pressing), are Jura's most unique offerings.

Domaine Rolet, the region's second-largest vineyard, has a pleasing shop/tasting room across from the Arbois town hall, as do many other wine sellers along the same street.

vinegar, and brewers of beer could not maintain consistent quality or taste. In 1858 Pasteur discovered that sterilization of beer, wine, and milk by heating at moderate temperature, for only a minute, would protect them, a process that became known as "Pasteurization."

You can visit Pasteur's home and laboratory in Arbois. He lived here from the time he was eleven, and summered here for the rest of his life. His distillation equipment is still in the lab, and the house bathroom (Pasteur was a fiend for hygiene, of course), extremely rare for the time, remains intact. A favorite dish prepared regularly in the kitchen for his staff of ten to twenty assistants? Chicken soup! Don't miss the utterly modern, easy-to-clean linoleum carpet from 1895.

Saline Royale, Arc et Senans

Built rapidly between 1775 and 1779 by the visionary Claude-Nicolas Ledoux, the **Royal Salt Works** was designed to be a working marvel of industrial architecture, an Enlightenment-inspired project that combined the works with a planned city for its workers. The salt works itself operated as intended only for about ten years and the planned city was never built. Today the handsome saltworks is a UNESCO World Heritage Site that Thomas Jefferson would have felt at home in.

Maison de Louis Pasteur, Arbois

As a young boy Louis Pasteur delighted primarily in two things—fishing and drawing. By the time he was a college student, his portraits of friends and family were gaining him acclaim. An uninspired student in his early years, chemistry finally grabbed his attention and never let go. The portraitist became the nineteenth century's most influential scientist, founder of the germ theory of disease, developer of vaccines against anthrax and rabies, and hero to the wine, beer and, okay, milk producers of France. Pasteur's private vineyard was near Arbois.

In Pasteur's day, fermentation did not always steer a steady course—wine went sour, vinegar failed to become

Distillerie Armand Guy, Pontparlier

The fabled Pernod drink made from absinthe, herbs, and anise seed, the drink known as "The Green Fairy" that made wackos of Verlaine, Van Gogh, Lautrec, and many others, packed an alcohol wallop, between sixty-five and seventy-two percent. Absinthe-drinking protocol demanded that ice water drip slowly from a vat onto sugar placed in a special spoon spanning the glass, the mix then falling into the Pernod to cause that charming milky look.

Some reports indicate that absinthe that is brewed from alcohol derived from beets, potatoes, or grains (as compared to grapes) can lead to assorted difficulties; whether or not the absinthe ingredient itself caused hallucinations, drink one or two of these and you would be well pickled anyway. Pernod ruled the absinthe roost until an enormous fire in 1901 at their Pontparlier factory caused a huge depletion in stocks; fortunately, an alert factory worker began dumping vatsful of Pernod into the river Doubs to save the town from being blown up. The locals, sensing a free absinthe bonanza, raced to the green river's edge and began drinking up the liquid in their hats. At the advent of World War I, absinthe fell into further disfavor and was banned in 1915.

You can visit this former absinthe factory, which since 1921 has produced only distilled anise seed. The oak vats once held absinthe, and you can view the alembics through which "the green fairy" once flowed.

Note: absinthe was never illegal in the UK and is once again legal in the EU, though the amount of thujone allowed is maxed at 10 mg. (Curiously, thujone is a naturally occurring chemical compound commonly found in many plants, particularly herbs and spices.) In the US absinthe is not allowed but a variety of companies sell absinthe online.

Musée des Maisons Comtoises, Nancray

Twenty-five Franche-Comté buildings from the seventeenth to the nineteenth centuries have been rebuilt on this thirty-five-acre site, where visitors can take in the architecture and also view bread baking, old garden varieties, animal action, and butter and cheese making. One 1794 farmhouse here boasts what is called a *tue*, a huge pyramidal chimney that covers much of the house and in which sausages of the region were smoked.

Northeast:
Alsace, Lorraine, Champagne-Ardennes, Nord

Truly there was a northern feel here. Alsace, its rich Rhine farmland making up the territory with which both Germany and France have played tug of war, is the region of sausage and *sauerkraut*, and of dishes made from Belgian endive. Its local cafés have long lists of beers, many of them Belgian and German, as well as the more typically sweet white wines of the region. Lorraine and Champagne are France's northern-most wine-producing areas. And this is *frites* country. The finest twice-fried potatoes, now found all over France, originated in the north, with cattle providing the beef tallow that once flavored these golden brown potatoes. Cold beers refresh the hot summers and hot, cabbagey soups warm the snowy winters.

But all is not mountain country here. Looking out the windows of the **Grand Hôtel de la Reine** in Nancy after a restful sleep undisturbed by the ghost of Marie Antoinette (she had slept there, too), we decided over sliced ham and coddled eggs that the view of elegant Stanislas Square was the best from a breakfast room thus far in France. And we were soon to discover the contributions of a real son of the Northeast, Poland's Count Stanislas, to France's food heritage.

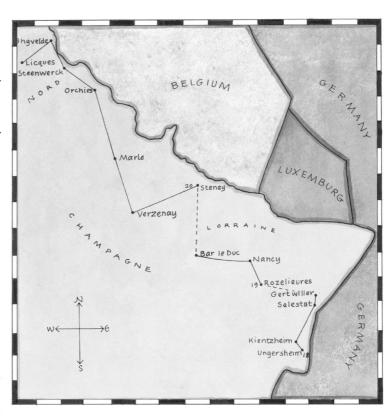

Stage 18: Ungersheim to Kientzheim to Selestat to Gertwiller

On the lookout for cabbage, sweet and sour, the region's sweeter white wines, hearty bread, and warm spice cake fresh from the oven

Ecomusée d'Alsace, Ungersheim

This is as close to a living museum of the cabbage family we have ever seen. One of Europe's finest open air museums, the Ecomusée covers much more than cabbage, of course, and yet Alsace's most famous food does deserve this kind of thorough examination. The English word "cabbage" derives from the now slangy French word *caboche,* meaning head, and has been a staple since the Celts were wandering about giving their cabbage word, *bresic,* to the Romans who turned it into *Brassica,* the botanical name of the entire cabbage family.

The gardens here grow every variety of cabbage imaginable—early, middle, and late; red, purple, green, and variegated (there are hundreds of varieties in the world)—as well as its derivatives, such as rutabaga, broccoli, and cauliflower.

The guides demonstrate the process of turning fermented cabbage into a famous French comfort food, sauerkraut, eaten with tasty sausages, apple sauce, egg noodles, or potatoes. You can eat and drink heartily at the museum's tavern, and then put up at its inn.

Walk through three hundred years of Alsace domestic architecture (the oldest house dates from 1529), meet the Gascony race of pigs popular here in the eighteenth century, and experience farm life and traditions, including an exceptional collection of carts.

Musée du Vignoble et des Vins d'Alsace, Kientzheim

More than ninety percent of Alsatian wines are white, and of those, most are produced from two varieties, the Riesling and Pinot Blanc grapes. Their story and that of the bottle makers, barrel makers, and viticulturists of this region are told here. The jewel of the collection is a 1716 wine press.

5. — Presse continue à vis d'Archimède, de Mabille.

Maison du Pain d'Alsace, Selestat

A bread museum built around a modern functioning bakery, in which you can observe, take lessons, and, of course, taste, this enterprise is established in a building that has been the headquarters of the local Bakers Association since 1522.

Musée du Pain d'Épices et des Douceurs d'Autrefois, Gertwiller

Sweet bread made from flour, honey, and sugar was a product of the monasteries in this region, starting about the twelfth century. By the sixteenth century the spices brought back from assorted Crusades began to have their way with this simple sweet cake, transforming it into the *pain d'épices* of today. Cinnamon, clove, anise, nutmeg, and ginger became the stars, with candied citrus and nuts playing supporting roles. Michel Habsiger, owner of the Lips spice cake operation, has been collecting artifacts pertaining to Alsace folk life, baking, candy making, and such since he was fifteen. His 10,000-piece collection, jammed into a small but colorful space, is the core of the exhibition here that explains the traditions of this typical cake through molds and utensils galore, typical furnishings, and baking gear.

65

Stage 19: Rozelieures to Nancy to Bar le Duc

Nancy

Though we never actually ate Quiche Lorraine here in its supposed birthplace, we did discover that the dish has been recognized since the eleventh century, and that it was always considered peasant fare.

Nancy is known for the gilded square created by and named after Count Stanislas, but the full import of the eighteenth-century Count's gifts to cuisine are less well known. Stanislas, a Polish king whose daughter married Louis XV of France, was installed in Nancy in 1738 to look after the King's Lorraine holdings. The Count was apparently stout and famous for his bad breath. Still, he was lavishly looked after by the ladies, one of whom conspired with the Count's chef to come up with the oddly flavored Bergamot candies that not only sweetened the Count's breath but also put Nancy on the hard candy map.

Bergamot is a citrus originating in Asia but widely grown in Calabria, Italy. The unique odor of its peel flavors Earl Grey tea, famous colognes, and Bergamot candies.

The Oxford Companion to Food does not necessarily agree with the next Count Stanislas story. The Count was fond of a yeasty cake from his homeland known as *kugelhopf*, but as

he was getting on, and his teeth couldn't handle anything too substantial, his cook decided to soften the cake by moisturizing it with rum. The result? *Baba au rhum*, so named because the Count's bedside reading was *Ali Baba and the Forty Thieves*. However, a cake known as baba had long existed in Poland, the Count's homeland, so the Ali Baba touch simply may have appealed to the Count's pleasure in "double entendre."

And finally, the Madeleine. The portly Count's cook Madeleine Paulmier came up with the idea for the shell-shaped biscuits while the Stanislas household was in residence at Commercy about 1775. Pleased with the cookies, King Louis XV, the Count's son-in-law, named them for the cook. Rumors are unfounded that the young cook's shapely body was the model for the statue of Neptune's wife in a fountain at one corner of Stanislas' magnificent square in Nancy. The lady depicted there is in fact Madame Marie de Boufflers, Stanislas' longtime mistress. Commercy is still a center of Madeleine production.

The Madeleine took on new life after Marcel Proust wrote of dipping one into his lime flower *tisane* (a herbal tea), the taste then sending him back to childhood in his aunt's kitchen in Illiers-Combray.

Maison de la Mirabelle, Rozelieures

Sometime during the fifteenth century a yellow plum from the Middle East arrived in Lorraine, where it stayed and thrived, not venturing much beyond this region. The *mirabelle* is a local favorite for jams, pastry fillings, and *eau de vie*, but eaten fresh is not considered that satisfying.

Visit this producer to learn more, watch a video about the fruit and its processing, observe the distillery, and taste away.

Musée Lorrain, Nancy

Situated in the ducal palace in the oldest part of Nancy, this museum is comprised of several parts, but one ticket suffices for all. One section devoted to everyday life features kitchens on display: a sixteenth-century mantle-free cooking hearth flanked by hooks from which to hang oil lamps; a nineteenth-century farm kitchen with a huge wooden cabbage cutter on legs and a wood table displaying all the tools a pig would not want to be near; and carts, wagons, tools, and oil paintings capturing rural life and food preparation.

In another wing, feast your eyes on the allegorical comic strip in five parts of a large, extremely well-preserved, sixteenth-century Flemish tapestry called *Condemnation of Banquet*. Banquet, it appears, is an unsavory glutton with a nasty sidekick, Supper, while Dinner is the worthy hero. The villains plot against him calling on Colic, Gout, and others. In panel four, Dame Experience acts as judge, with the aid of Diet. By the sixth panel, lost during the Revolution, Banquet and Supper evidently are vanquished and Dinner is restored as a hero. Truly a foodie's morality play.

Confitures à la Lorraine, Bar-le-Duc

You could probably bet that only in France would there still exist workers, all of them women, willing to gently extract seven seeds from one red currant after another, using a goose quill, a mere three hours of labor for two pounds of fruit. But in Bar le Duc red currant jam, sometimes known as "Caviar of the Bar," has been a coveted luxury item since the fourteenth century, and a favorite of Victor Hugo's in the nineteenth century. Today only one processer of the old school is still in production. Anne Detriez, the owner, learned the business from her grandfather.

Stage 20: *Stenay to Verzenay to Marle to Orchies to Steenwerck to Ghyvelde to Licques*

The libations of northern France abound along this route, including head-clearing chicory, all enjoyed with the filling foods of French Flanders.

Musée Européene de la Biére, Stenay

This may be the only place in the world where you can view a collection of 8,000 *sous-bocks*, the disposable coasters that breweries print up and distribute to their customers. Mostly from France, Belgium, Germany, and England, the *sous-bocks* were a gift of one collector to this museum that is close to the Belgian border. Set up in a former malt house, the museum covers the world of European beer on three floors.

Le Phare de Verzenay en Champagne, Verzenay

Grapes make their last stand here in France, on the high plains of Champagne, which is even more northerly than the vineyards of Alsace. The short growing season of this cold climate led to the refermentation of wine in the bottle, which produces carbon dioxide bubbles. The seventeenth-century Benedictine monk Dom Perignon of the Abbey at Hautvillers did not really invent champagne—in fact the bubbles in his community's wine were something he tried to eradicate, to no avail. His methods of blending various grape juices, however, and selecting stronger bottles made in England that might not explode as easily, among other techniques, certainly created the beginnings of the modern champagne industry.

Keeping an even higher vantage point is this remarkable museum built around a lighthouse. All of the museum is devoted to the subject of champagne—its origins, its soils, techniques, traditions, pleasures, tools, weather concerns, and so forth. The lighthouse was built in 1909 as a publicity stunt and to provide advertising space for a local wine merchant.

Le Musée des Temps Barbares et ses Journées Merovingiennes, Marle

Charlemagne's Frankish predecessors lived here during the sixth and seventh centuries, little knowing they were living in the Dark Ages, as they farmed, created pottery, made soup, and baked bread—and quite probably drank mead, honey-derived alcohol.

This Merovingian, partially open-air site preserves the architecture of that era, displays artifacts of the time, and also hosts special events where visitors, too, can quaff mead and behave in somewhat uncivilized fashion.

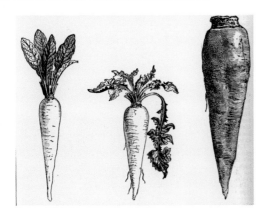

Maison de la Chicorée, Orchies

Chicory in France is a root that, ground and dried, makes a coffee substitute or additive and was once a medicinal staple. New Orleans coffee drinkers have long enjoyed chicory mixed into their dark brews. Chicory has no caffeine and imparts a chocolate-like taste to a brew—it may also lower cholesterol and stimulate the immune system.

This museum created by Leroux, the world's leading chicory producer, presents the apothecary side of the story, including antique ceramic utensils and pottery, but also presents the history of chicory marketing. Before instant coffee was invented, dried ground chicory stood in.

The same plant's young thick shoots, grown in the dark, produce green-tipped plump white delicacies known in many places as Belgian endive, though the French know them as *chicons*. The endive growers of Flanders often wrap them in ham and cook them in creamy cheese sauces.

Belgian endive is practically a brand-new plant, having been "discovered" about 1850. A professional gardener connected with the Brussels Botanical Garden took some wild chicory plants and grew them indoors in a cellar, with dirt mounded up around the base of them, perhaps inadvertently. An assistant, coming upon one such plant, was surprised to discover under the earth what the Belgians now call "white gold," a white-leafed elongated head with yellowish tips.

Musée de la Vie Rural, Steenwerck Ecomusée du Bommelaers Wall, Ghyvelde

These two museums offer a window into Flanders rural life, both featuring magnificent old kitchens. At Steenwerck you can visit the village grocery shop and witness the threshing of the wheat in the farm's courtyard.

Love "Belgian" waffles, rabbit pâté, "Belgian" endive, potatoes with everything? Visit the old French Flanders farm near Dunkirk and not only experience the golden days of farming but also eat well at the farm's family tables. You can also taste *La Chicorette*, a chicory-based aperitif.

69

Chicons à la Flamande

The snowy white endive, with its chartreuse tips, is now widely grown commercially in northern France and Belgium. Try this vegetable as it is eaten in homes across the region (this recipe reflects my own version of the dish):

Choose endive whose tips are tightly closed. Optionally, core out the very end of each endive before cooking.

6 or 8 Belgian endives
juice of one lemon
1 T. sugar
salt and pepper
4 T. butter
$^1/_4$ to $^1/_2$ c. water, as needed

3 hardboiled eggs
2 T. butter
chopped parsley

Melt butter in a heavy pot and add endives, sugar, lemon juice, salt, and pepper. Coat endives in butter, add a bit of water, and cover with a lid that fits well. The endives will steam nicely for about 50 minutes to an hour over low to medium heat. Once endives are tender, remove the lid, turn up the heat, and cook until butter/juice turns brown, rolling the endives over and over in the caramelizing sauce.

Serve hot, sprinkled with bits of hard boiled egg crumbled into remaining melted butter, topped with parsley.

Bommelaers is an award-winning *"musée fleuris,"* an untranslatable phrase that means the museum has a satisfying show of flowering trees and flower gardens.

For more experiences with the warmth of everyday Flanders, try one of the local taverns or *estaminets*. More homey and family-oriented perhaps than typical French cafés, the *estaminets* are gathering places where people not only enjoy beer and wine, but also card games, old wooden games, and long conversations. We stopped by one, **l'Estaminet 'T Kasteelhof**, in the hilltop town of Cassel, across from the eighteenth-century windmill. Perched on the edge of a steep hill, this cozy *estaminet*, its rafters festooned with hops, baskets, and country tin pitchers, offers about seventy local beers, and a lengthy menu of Flemish comfort foods.

Turkey Festival, Licques

America's own native fowl, the turkey, was brought here to what was once Spanish-dominated Flanders in the early eighteenth century. Monks of Licques Abbey obtained the birds from Spanish travelers and began raising them. Since then the locals have become famous for producing the finest French free range turkeys (the French eat almost as much turkey as North Americans). In the second week of December, many handsome birds are corralled each year to make their final lifetime waddle, down the main street, to the tunes of a brass band. After which they are strangled, plucked, stuffed, and roasted. Mark your calendar and be there.

Northwest:
Pas de Calais, Haute Normandie, Basse Normandie, Bretagne

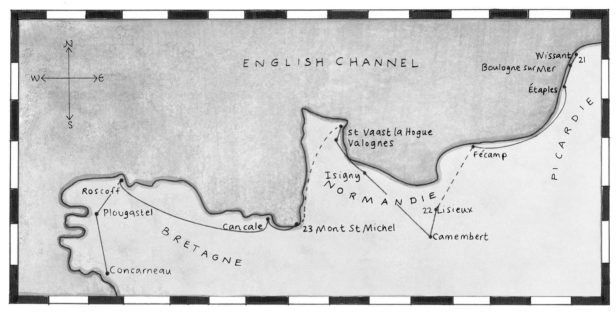

Rollo the Viking, also known as Rollo the Walker because his men could find no horse strong enough to carry him, was a codfish-eating marauder of the tenth century. In 911 he made a deal with the Franks—let me and my soldiers stay, I won't keep attacking Paris, and I'll be your vassal—and thus became the first Duke of Normandy. He and his fellow Norsemen, from Denmark and Norway, and their Norse women as well are the people after whom Normandy is named.

As the Vikings were prime cod purveyors from their Newfoundland waters, teaching the Basques, Bretons, and Normans the tricks of the trade, so cod joined with cows to create solid, satisfying northern food offerings, such as the finest butter on the planet. Buckwheat, too, played a role in these climes. A latecomer to France, in the mid-1500s hearty buckwheat found a toehold in the rocky poor soils of Brittany. Not a grass, but an Asian seed plant related to rhubarb, ground buckwheat seeds became the flour of choice for French pancakes. Buckwheat, rye, and oats, able to thrive in thin soils, are not well suited to bread making so the people developed a fondness for porridges and puddings, as well as pancakes. Buckwheat is sometimes called Sarazin flour in France, as it may have arrived either with one or another Arab incursion, or with Crusaders returning from the Middle East.

In front of the 16th c. building that houses the Ecomusée de la Pomme au Cidre in St. Maclou la Briére is a turn-of-the-century apple press that would have been turned by horse power.

Another northern food item well-rooted in both Normandy and Brittany is the apple, along with its immediate derived beverage, alcoholic cider, an export of France since before it was France—the Basques may have learned cider making from the northern sixth-century Gauls and passed on that knowledge to other people in other places. (William the Bastard, Rollo's descendant, made a quick hop across the Channel in 1066 in order to become an Englishman and, possibly, gain himself a more triumphant moniker. Evidently he carried some barrels of Norman cider with him, perhaps to compare his product to that of apple-abundant England.)

Both these regions of France reflect their northern maritime rainy climate of cool winters and mild summers, hearty foods, and closeness to the sea, as well as their ties to Great Britain, just across the Channel. (The cockles in the typical Norman/Breton *fruits de mer* overflowing the thin tray perched on a pedestal typically come from England—the English happily harvest the tiny shellfish, but evidently eat them only when on holiday in northern France.)

While we never actually found a Breton buckwheat flour *galette* that included dried salt cod, we thought the combo would make a tidy historical package.

(The Bretons do like cod with creamed mushrooms and bacon...) Perhaps somewhat over-fed after a few weeks on the road, we welcomed a chance to eat a simple meal of buckwheat *galettes* and cider in Brittany. We found them in a crisply nautical, narrow café called **Creperie-Glacier du Port de Plaisance**, in Concarneau, where "Anne et Florence vous accueillent." Anne's simplest *galettes*, folded into squares and topped with the best Normandy butter, were briskly delivered to our table by Florence, a woman easily able both to pour our cider and greet a regular customer, leaving us all feeling well attended to.

Stage 21: Wissant to Boulogne sur Mer to Etaples to Fecamp

This coastal area features Wissant, the last port in France where fishermen sell directly to the public. Their one-man boats known as *flobarts* are high bowed and brightly painted. Each August the tradition is celebrated in a Flobart Festival where visitors can try their hands at piloting their own *flobarts*.

In Boulogne you can walk into a tossing and pitching deep-sea trawler at the city's new Sea World-type museum, **Nausicaa.**

Mareis—Centre de la Pêche Artisanale, Etaples

This museum is all about modern fishing techniques and concerns regarding ocean pollution and dwindling fishing stocks; its exhibits also explain fish marketing (women always sold fish alongside the quay), tides, and how electronic gear make finding fish almost too easy. The museum is housed in a restored fishnet factory that once employed many wives of fishermen.

Musée des Terre-Nuevas et de la Pêche, Fécamp

Dedicated to the Normandy men who fished for cod off Newfoundland from 1520 more or less to the present day, this museum features compelling paintings as well as the expected fishing gear and models. It also pays homage to herring and mackerel. Herring was the first choice for Catholics, and a special favorite of priest-turned-satirist Rabelais. High-protein salted herring could be kept a year in tubs, so they were ideal for keeping armies fed. On February 12, 1429, at the Battle of the Herrings, French and Scottish troops tried unsuccessfully to steal herring supplies being convoyed to the English army attacking Orléans.

Not all Norman fishing was done by men—the women claimed beach fishing for themselves, wearing hobnailed boots called *galoches* and tossing out and hauling in nets with professional ease. They also supervised the smoking process, using the beech-chip fires that give herring its distinct flavor and color.

Smoking of the Herring, Etretat

Each November the enticing scent of the herring catch being smoked in traditional smoke houses attracts towns-people and visitors alike.

Palais Bénédictine, Fécamp

Alexandre le Grand's gigantic portrait dominates a wall in the ornate palace he had built in Fécamp. In 1863, le Grand found the sixteenth-century recipe for herby, bitter Benedictine liqueur in a book his ancestor had purchased in the eighteenth century. The mix had been concocted by a Venetian, Brother Bernardo Vincelli, assigned to the abbey at Fécamp, and was a favorite in France for years, dutifully turned out by the Benedictines until the chaos of the French Revolution ground things to a halt.

Le Grand tinkered with the formula somewhat, ulti-mately employing twenty-seven herbs from four conti-nents, and by 1873 had established a proper factory for its production. His dream, though, was to marry industry with art, by creating a building that could house both the dis-tillery and his massive art collection.

(Look for a favorite foodie painting here, the sixteenth-century Flemish piece titled *The Good Rich*, showing self-sat-isfied white-ruffed burghers handing coin-embedded, hearty bread to the supplicant poor. For hellfire and damnation see *The Wicked Rich*.)

Opened in 1888, the business continues today. An entire hall is devoted to the promotional efforts of Benedictine, an advertising art bonanza.

This exuberant, over-the-top museum inventively dis-plays and explains the twenty-seven ingredients and where they come from—Mace! Hyssop! Myrrh! Even *Piment langue d'oiseau* from Central Africa—and also invites you down below to tour the stills and caves—and, at the end, to blink into the light and begin tasting.

We have read that in 1937 a New York City barkeep was

the first to combine Benedictine with Cognac in a cocktail, to create the popular drink B&B, a concept the company swiftly picked up on, long since their most popular export to the U.S. No whisper of this turns up in Fécamp, howev-er. The original Benedictine beverage did begin, after all, with distilled brandy.

Warning: As you leave the shop, a discreet sign reads: "Please leave the Benedictine Palace with caution." No mat-ter how calmed you are by your free libations, be sure to stick your head out and take a good look to the left. The door opens directly—no curb, no sidewalk—into an actual street, featuring actual speeding cars.

Stage 22: Lisieux to Camembert to Isigny to Valognes to St Vaast la Hogue

Cows and Calvados, buttered hot cider, and a gourmande's grocer.

Le Domaine St. Hippolyte, Lisieux

Happy Norman cows with the distinctive brown circles around their eyes live here. You can view them, munching their hay, from up above on the second floor of the modern stable of the seventy-hectare, fifteenth-century manor. The land is farmed by a cooperative organized in 1995 to reinvigorate the Norman breed. Milking of course leads to cheese and butter making, and the *fromagerie* next door has see-through windows where visitors observe the steps in making both the thirteenth-century star *Pont l'Evêque* as well as *Livarot*, two of Normandy's most famous cheeses. The manor features some basic exhibits in outbuildings as well.

A gem on the property—a handsome pigeon tower in the Norman style.

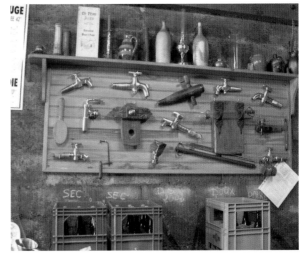

Le Père Jules, Saint-Desir-de Lisieux

Many regional processors of apples into cider and Calvados (apple brandy) offer tours and tastings. We visited **Père Jules Calvados**, a family business since 1919, where in season about eight people turn sixty-nine varieties of apple into apple brandy and *pommeau de Normandie*, a perfect mix of the first press of apple juice and Calvados, aged together for three to four years. (*Pommeau* was strictly a farm beverage, not allowed to be sold commercially until laws were changed in the twentieth century.) Traditionally Calvados itself is made from the prior year's cider, double-distilled over a wood fire. The Père Jules place offers a video in French, English, or German on apple and cider production, as well as a look around the distillery operation. The old oak-wood barrels gleam in the cave, and the tasting bar reminded us of an old Irish pub.

Vache normande
(Variété cotentine)

La Ferme Président, Camembert
Maison du Camembert, Camembert
Musée de Camembert, Vimoutiers

Cheese country from the mid-sixteenth century on, the legend of the "inventor" of Camembert lives on here. During the French Revolution farmer Marie Harel of Camembert gave refuge to a priest from Brie, and he in turn gave Marie the secret to improving her cheese-making skills. Research indicates Marie may have given the cheese its famous thick rind. By the end of the nineteenth century, thanks to both the innovative round poplar wood packaging conceived of by an engineer named Ridel, and the increasing power of rail travel to carry goods throughout France, Camembert became arguably France's most popular and famous cheese. It has inspired poets, painters, and sportsmen, one of whom initiated the Camembert toss—current record, forty meters—presumably making use of the runniest contenders.

You can take a look at **Beaumoncel**, Marie's farm, up the hill from **La Ferme Président**, a collection of Norman buildings containing a fine museum of Camembert by a major French producer, Président. You can see what Marie's *laiterie* must have been like, as well as learn the modern techniques of Camembert production, and taste away.

While *Camembert* is an AOC cheese produced in several industrial factories in France, you can still buy a local handmade version here.

Across the street is a Normandy specialties shop and info center, the **House of Camembert**, built in the shape of the famous round box.

The Camembert Museum in the nearby town of Vimoutiers, though not as up to date as the Président exhibition, has a remarkable collection of labels and advertising materials. Marie's statue in Vimoutiers lost its head due to Allied bombing runs in 1944. A new and rededicated statue was erected across from the town hall, thanks to the efforts of the American Borden Cheese company. Fortunately, a hard-working Norman cow, too, is honored in bronze.

Isigny-Sainte-Mère Butter Factory

The glories of Norman butter—buttercup yellow and tinged with a hint of hazelnut, as the Isigny press people say—can not only be tasted on your morning baguette but also seen up close and personal during the Isigny Tour.

200 million liters of milk a year are here converted into *crème fraîche*, butter, and cheese, even an AOC handmade *Camembert*.

Camembert Gratin

This easy spin on potato gratin makes use of half a Camembert, the other half to be munched on while slicing the potatoes.

Serves 4

1 kilo or 2.25 lbs potatoes
1 cup cream
1 $^1/_3$ c. milk
half a Camembert cheese
salt and pepper to taste

Peel potatoes and slice them thinly. Layer them in a buttered oven-proof dish.

Place the cheese, cream, and milk together in a sauce pan and gently heat until cheese begins to melt. Place the mix in a blender and, keeping the lid firmly in place, blend together on low.

Pour blended ingredients on top of the potatoes. Season with salt and pepper and bake in a moderate oven, 300 degrees F, for about 50 minutes.

Recipe Courtesy Isigny-Ste-Mere.

Musée Regional du Cidre, Valognes

The Gauls were apple eaters and cider drinkers long before the Romans arrived and began to eat the fruits as vegetables in soups and stews. (The apple is thought to be Eurasia's oldest fruit, with domesticated varieties enjoyed in ancient Egypt and Rome.) The apple's northern need for at least two months of hibernation made it the perfect fruit for Normandy and environs. Whether originating here or an idea lifted from the Basques of Biscay, cider making was well established by the eleventh century here, far more popular than beer. (*Cidre* in France is alcoholic apple juice, as compared to the fresh-pressed apple cider favorite of North American children each autumn.)

Installed in a fifteenth-century dyer's house, the museum still retains a narrow commode built into the stone, lodged cozily next to the fireplace, and with a fine natural-plumbing view out the arrow-loop window to the river below.

A food-related element, yes, but such a facility is not the focus of the fine collection that begins by explaining Norman cider making with an excellent thirteen-minute film.

Not a building for the handicapped, the museum has twelve rooms on several floors, filled with barrels, pottery crocks, glass bottles, presses of all ages and sizes, tableaus of Normans in daily life involved with cider and Calvados preparations, and more. Room 11 contains the most remarkable item of all—a bed carved from an 1831 cider barrel by the mischievous Louis Delhay sometime in the twentieth century. (The guide called this "Diogenes' barrel," a reference to the fourth-century BC Cynic philosopher's occasional habitat in Athens.) Delhay carved assorted ancient scenes, including, of course, Adam and Eve's encounter with the apple, and carefully transformed the barrel's spout into the shape of Adam's folly, so to speak.

The cider museum suggests this old Norman recipe to ward off a cold. Toast a piece of bread. Break it into bits and toss it into a jar of hot cider. Sweeten with honey and top with a healthy dose of Calvados. Drink.

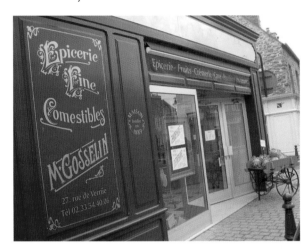

Épicerie Gosselin, St Vaast la Hogue

The English-French connection continues in the upscale yachting port of La Hogue, where we watched fishermen baiting their lines, their fingers black with the inky response of the protesting squid. (In 1692 the British and Dutch navies combined forces to whip Louis XIV's fleet near here, thereby containing the French, and squelching their effort to restore Catholic James II as king of England.)

A block away, just off the marina, is the Zabar's or Harrod's food hall of Normandy, a picnic lover's treasure trove, **Epicerie Gosselin**; they are purveyors to the yachting crowd, many from Britain, and to well-heeled customers who own houses nearby. Outside the door was parked a green-painted iron cart overflowing with the prettiest of *choux fleur*, the day's special. The store was founded in 1889 by Clovis

Gosselin, and today is run by the family's fourth generation. Eighteen employees hover nicely in the labyrinthine environs, stacked high with the Épicerie's house label goods, and fresh food and cheese displays. It's also a mini museum—featuring a two-hundred-year-old portable coffee roaster, ancient bottles of wine locked in glass cases, and other goodies.

Stage 23: *Mont St Michel to Cancale to Roscoff to Plougastel to Concarneau*

Omelets, oysters, and onions, sampled with strawberries and seafood.

The Celtic people who left Britain with the arrival of the Saxons came to Armorica, the Land Beyond the Sea, an isolated leg of land, and made it their own. The Bretons remain an isolated people with a unique language still spoken by some, the only Celtic speakers on the Continent.

Restaurant de la Mère Poulard, Mont St Michel

In 1888 Annette Poulard established her inn here and quickly became known for her exceptionally fluffy omelets. The secret? There are two, in fact: the separate whisking of the egg whites in copper bowls, and then the baking of the folded omelets in a wood-fired oven. You can stand outside and watch the slightly hokey ceremonial beating of the egg whites, or you can dine in, try to get a table that avails a view of the main event, and pay what some consider to be too much for an omelet, however lofty (and in one instance, frankly, runny).

La Ferme Marine, Cancale

Oysters were more plentiful here back in the days when John Singer Sargent painted his *Oyster Gatherers of Cancale*, women and children with large baskets on their hips, standing in wooden clogs on the hard sand wet from the receding tide, just about to begin the harvest. Still, the family business of **La Ferme** continues to produce and process oysters, offering visitors a tour of their operation, as well as an exhibition about their favorite bivalve. Tastings, too.

Sauce à l'Échalote

A simple dish really, but it makes oyster eating truly French. It's their version of a dipping sauce. Finely chop 2 small shallots and mix them with a good wine vinegar and a generous grinding of black pepper. Dab onto freshly opened oysters, and let them slide down. Don't forget the bread.

Maison du Johnnies, Roscoff

A pink onion, first grown from Portuguese seeds by a monk here in the middle of the seventeenth century, has been the cash crop of some enterprising Bretons for generations. The tasty bulb, full of vitamin C, warded off scurvy for Roscoff fishermen, away at sea for many weeks. Then in 1828 a grower named Henri Olivier decided to take some braided pinks across the Channel to Britain, selling them door to door, at first on foot, then by bike and eventually automobile. His success invigorated others to follow and the beret-wearing *Petit Jeans*, Little Johns, or Johnnies as they were quickly dubbed by their new customers, started a tradition that only dwindled out with World War II. Today only about fifteen Johnnies continue the trade, but a museum opened in summer 2004 is devoted to the entire story.

Roscoff growers hope their onion will proudly carry the AOC label by 2005. Look for an onion festival here the end of August. An Algerian omelet would happily embrace the pale pink Johnny—it combines beaten egg with thinly sliced onions sautéed in olive oil and fennel seed, along with fresh chopped mint.

Musée de la Fraise et du Patrimonie— Plougastel

Europe had its own native strawberries and for years these were well appreciated by the Royals who could afford them, eaten either with cream by the ladies, or wine by the gentlemen. A berry from the American northeast, Virginia, was imported in the seventeenth century and added to the mix. Then in 1714, a Breton ship's engineer named, impossibly, Frézier (rhymes with *fraisier*), brought back several strawberry plants from the Pacific coast of South America, boasting of their huge pineapple-scented fruits. Glorious though they may have been, the plants never gave again, and for thirty years there they sat.

In 1740 Frézier evidently carried some plants to Brest, where an unknown hero of food history put the Virginia berry plant next to the so-called Chilean berry. Mother Nature then worked her magic to produce the variety of strawberry now most grown around the world. By 1766 markets of Brest were selling the new hybrid regularly.

You can learn the history of the first Plougastel strawberry, enter a nineteenth-century farmstead and see the locals cleaning strawberries, watch a film about strawberry history, and take a tour of the strawberry's world story at this museum, also focused on the other traditions of the region.

Note: Certain Internet sources claim that the French *fraise* was named after Frézier (not true), that he produced the hybrid (no), and that he lived in Plougastel (probably not). Nonetheless the town became a strawberry power and still celebrates a strawberry festival in June.

Biscuiterie François Garrec, Benodet

A family business since the nineteenth century, **Garrec** invites visitors to witness the work of pastry chefs as they hand-make the thin and delectable biscuits and crêpes typical of Brittany. The entire operation, including quality control and packaging, is clearly visible through windows.

Musée de la Pêche, Concarneau

A retired fishing boat is tied up to the pier, the voices of the crew coming on as you move about, giving you the sense that the men just stepped off for a drink. Yellow oilskins hang at the ready, and large wicker baskets await the next catch. And yet there really is no fishy smell on board.

It's the *Hermerica*, built at St Nazaire in 1957, home to eleven men for fifteen-day stretches along the Irish Coast. She was at sea until 1981, pulling in cod, sea bream, sole, and more. Now she's tied up at the pier near the fish museum, and if you're willing and nimble enough to clamber up into a tower, then cross over into another one, and walk some slippery steps—you can reach it.

This must-see museum, built into the old fortress walls, displays beautifully made and lighted wooden models of boat building, fish smoking, salt processing and the tinning of sardines, among other displays. A favorite artifact was an old pair of fisherman's *sabots*, wooden shoes topped with handmade canvas and leather. The museum informs us that rubber boots were not developed until the close of the 1930s. The hard, cold, wet life of fisher people and those who processed their bounty is well expressed here.

West:
Pays de la Loire, Poitou-Charentes, Aquitaine

You can't eat the bright white light out in the Marais Salants, the salt marshes of the Guérande—from the Breton *Gwen Ran*, or "white land"—though maybe it's bottled up in the flashing bubbles of the champagne you drink as you sniff the salty sea essence of the local oysters, before sliding them down the throat. The houses here are white or pastel, the sun bounces off the flats with a not unpleasant glare, and even the salt workers themselves, traditionally at least, wear white breeches.

Here in the west, a rainy, marshy lowland region where temperatures are mild year-round, salt is the primary element, historically linked with oysters and fishing, and both linked as well with cognac and the Dutch, Flemish, and English traders who helped turn the slow but steady wine trade into the international boom. Even within France salt was a traded commodity—Bretons exchanged their salt for the wheat and herring of the Normans.

Salt is not just a happy condiment, it is an essential life ingredient, and the primary means of preserving both food and drink before refrigeration. To the Romans it was one more good reason to invade Gaul. In the sixteenth century the insidious salt tax was extended to the western parts of France, causing active revolts. According to French food historian Maguelonne Toussaint-Samat, the rabble of Bordeaux evidently grabbed the bureaucrat who administered the tax, cut him up, and salted his parts, much as they would have ministered to a fattened pig. And by the time of the Revolution, the then centuries-old salt tax, mixed with famine after

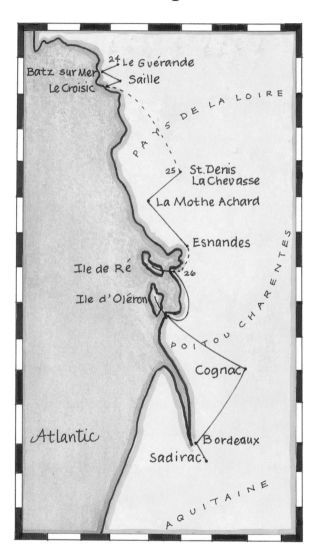

a poor grain harvest, was a further incitement to overthrow the aristocracy, who, naturally, paid no salt tax.

Salt, too, we discovered not only has color—gray salt is the most reminiscent of the sea—but also perfume. Experts can apparently sniff out the difference among salt from mines, salt of the sea, sea salt skimmed first from the surface of the flats, and salt from below, slower to appear after evaporation. My nose for salt was sadly undeveloped, though a faintly brackish, slightly geranium-leaved aromatic scent did begin to take vague olfactory shape.

Potato specialities from the Hôtel Restaurant l'Ocean, Le Bois Plage.

Stage 24: Le Guérande to Batz sur Mer to Saille to Le Croisic

A remarkable union of three separate salt-related institutions comprises what we would call a salt museum, perhaps the finest in the world. And make sure to fill up on both fact and folklore about seagoing mussels and land-based snails. For dessert, biscuits.

The first we visited in Pradel, **Terre de Sel**, an enterprise begun by a cooperative of salt producers, was out in the flats, with a black-painted hanger of a building that could not have provided a better introduction to the subject. While the local story of the seasons of the *paludiers*, the salt workers, is their primary focus, you also can observe the differences between salt from Greece, Austria, Djibouti, and Japan and perhaps for the first time discover that salt, too, has perfume.

June to September is the season of the hand-harvesting time here, with wind, rain, and sun itself the enemy. From the building's balcony you can see out over the flats and take walking tours, either with a naturalist or a salt worker, by prior arrangement with the cooperative. A well-stocked shop sells the wares of the co-op members.

Musée des Marais Salants, Batz sur Mer

One of the oldest folk art museums in Brittany, set up in 1887, this is the second in the trio of salt-related museums. It relates the archaeological history of salt production. The Gauls used to boil away the salt water with fires in the first century, and from the ninth century monks of the Guérande were working the flats. The museum also introduces the everyday life of the *paludiers* who labored with salt in the eighteenth and nineteenth centuries.

The people of old Batz are here, in their vivid lilac and red outfits, always worn over white, and the men's handsome yet almost absurdly huge dark hats. Their homes always featured heavy, carved furniture colored blood red, *sang de boeuf,* a term meaning "oxblood" in French.

Each kitchen held a huge clay pot containing at least one, sometimes two pigs preserved in salt, inside the huge fireplace were benches whose cavities stored salt, and an unusual triangular wood *porte-chaudron* held the cooking pot from which people ate. Every household, too, valued its cache of salted sardines.

Maison des Paludiers, Saille

The ecological, natural, meteorological story of salt is here—introduced by a brilliant film that shows humans as the salt-dependent sea creatures we once were. Salt still flows naturally in our bodies, hence our continuing daily need for it, especially in our brain and kidneys. The animated film goes on to recount the role of salt throughout history.

We discussed global warming and the coming ice age with the guide, whose parting words were, "ah well, better to live with enthusiasm than with fear." And a pinch of salt.

Moules à la Crème

Clean the mussels by scrubbing them well with a brush in cold water and then removing with a sharp knife the "beard," that little gizmo that looks like an errant piece of seaweed sticking out from the shell. (Some shy from removing the beard as it does seem to offend the still living mollusk. Sometimes I leave the beard alone.) Throw out the mussels that stay open even when you try to close them up again by hand.

1 kilo or about 2 lbs of mussels per person
chopped garlic, shallots, and onion, as well as 2 celery stalks, to cover the bottom of a large pot
fresh parsley and thyme, or dried versions of same, but more of it
1 T. butter
1 1/2 c. dry white wine
cream to please tastes

Sauté the garlic, shallot, onion, and celery in butter, but do not brown. Add the wine, herbs, and mussels. Steam them for 3–5 minutes. Shake the pot to mix well the veggies, broth, and mussels.

Place a tablespoon of cream in each bowl, serve up mussels, broth, and veggies. (Eliminate the mussels that are shut tight.) Eat with crusty bread and more dry white wine, or cold blond beer.

Maison de la Mytiliculture, Tréhiguier

The local "farmers of the sea" raise mussels, a tasty alternative to oysters, and a product of this town since the nineteenth century. The mussels are raised on nets extended between stakes, or *buchots*, a method of farming said to have originated with an Irishman named Patrick Walton shipwrecked near La Rochelle in 1235. But again, the industrious Gauls were probably raising mussels in beds well before that. This exhibition in an 1881 lighthouse on the history and methods of local mussel farming will send you racing to the nearest bistro for *moules marinières* with *frites*, a delectable dish also a favorite of the Belgians, mixing dry white wine, garlic, shallots, and the freshest of plump mussels.

Le Moulin de la Falaise, Batz sur Mer

If you had a Euro for every French place name that includes *moulin*, you would be very rich indeed. The Babylonians pumped water using windmills about 4,000 years ago, but the use of wind power to grind grain came later, and may not have reached France until the eleventh century. Under the creaking arms of this restored sixteenth-century windmill, near the sea where the wind almost always blows, you can buy the freshly ground organic buckwheat flour of the miller himself, Xavier Phulpin. His recipe of flour, Guérande salt, an egg, and water, well stirred, makes fine *galettes*.

Biscuiterie des Marais

If you want to satisfy your food history needs while you shop, this is the place. You can examine the Biscuiterie's huge collection of Breton antique biscuit tins, as well as buy authentic tools used for making *galettes*, and any of a zillion different salts and salt holders, as well as biscuits.

Espace Escargots, Le Croisic

Before they hit the butter and parsley, snails lead a pleasant life. You can observe them through windows at this snail farm, view a film all about snail raising, and then, taste.

Stage 25: St Denis la Chevasse to La Mothe Achard to Esnandes

The Vendée, birthplace of Eleanor of Aquitaine, and site of a bloody civil war after the French Revolution in which the mainly Catholic peasants of the Vendée used their scythes and other farm implements as weapons (they lost), today thrives on agriculture, the sea, and tourism.

Le Musée des Ustensiles de Cuisine Ancien, St Denis la Chevasse

All the fine, even fabled, French ingredients in the garden or in the markets must, in the end, be grated, mashed, ground up, cooked up, sautéed, simmered, roasted, grilled, or baked. This most unusual museum preserves and displays what people used to cook with from 1850 through the 1960s.

And while the early-era cast iron stoves and copper implements are striking, we were especially grabbed by the aluminum room. Bauxite, after all, from which aluminum is derived, was named after the village Les Baux de Provence in southern France, where geologist Pierre Berthier first discovered it in 1821. But it wasn't until the late 1880s that engineers discovered how to make actual aluminum. The heyday of the thin, easily heat-conducting metal was from the 1920s into the 1950s. (The demand for aluminum during World War II ended its dominance in the kitchen as stainless steel took over.)

The museum's most prized aluminum item is a tandem saucepan, on which you could cook two different items at the same time, given a large enough burner. There's something for every cook here—a 1910 egg beater, an eighteenth-century waffle iron, a 1913 pressure cooker that was almost guaranteed to blow up (took them forty years to perfect the pressure cooker), and a French army officer's kitchen trunk, complete with corkscrews, china and glassware, recipes, appropriate cookware, linens—sigh. *Vive la France!*

Looking down on the perfect order of a French officer's kitchen trunk.

Le Potager Extraordinaire, La Mothe Achard

It all started with Michel Rialland's collection of over three hundred squashes and gourds and today it's a major biodiversity garden, open to the public, and comprising nineteen themed garden displays. Some visitors never make it out of the extensive shop.

La Maison de la Mytiliculture, Esnandes

This new installation about mussels culture in the **Marais Poitevin** illustrates well the biology of this bivalve, as well as its history here.

Stage 26: Île de Ré to Île d'Oléron to Cognac to Bordeaux to Sadirac

Potatoes and oysters, cognac and wine, then on veggies dine.

Many of us could live happily on oysters, potatoes, wine, and a bit of salt. Especially if we could walk by the sea and go to market in villages whose streets overflow with hollyhocks in summer, and whose white houses all uniformly feature green shutters. The locals say the color originated from fishermen doing up their shutters with dark green left over from painting their boats' hulls.

The Île de Ré, today a causeway away from the old Protestant stronghold of La Rochelle, prospered until about 1832 when the *phylloxera* plague hit their vineyards, competition compromised their salt sales, and cholera began killing off the population.

Today summer visitors, oysters, and AOC potatoes, the first in France, have revitalized the area. *"La terre, la mer, et l'air"*—earth, sea, and air combine to produce the early potatoes of Ré, five varieties which share the AOC seal. The potato, a Peruvian native, is revered in France—the country produces about 140 different varieties of potatoes and its chefs at most cooking schools must pass a potato preparation test to achieve their diplomas.

The *primeurs* or new potatoes of Ré have a slightly sweet, earthy taste much appreciated by local restaurant chefs. The potatoes cannot be sold after July 31 or before April 20, and the local festival in their honor is May 20 in Le Bois Plage.

The restaurant at **Hôtel Restaurant L'Ocean** in Le Bois Plage, run by Anne and Frederic Latour, happily offers several potato dishes, and we tried them all. As well as sardines served with *tapenade*, and an Île specialty, *dos de cabillaud en écailles de pomme de terre*, cod covered with

"fish scales" and thinly sliced, crisply baked potatoes. For dessert they suggested *Jonchee Charentaise à la Confiture de Feouil*, an extremely regional country dish. It's goat's cheese in a roll, topped with cream, cognac, and fennel jam. The hotel itself is utterly elegant, simple, comfortable, and pleasing.

Any of the oyster sellers on the Île will supply you with the finest *fines* and *speciales de claire*, but the people at *Ets Demanliere* are especially cordial and friendly. Charles gave us a tour of his family business and supplied us with a particular knife used in oyster farming, while his mother set up the adjacent restaurant for the day's customers.

Fort Royer Site Ostreicole et Naturel, Saint Pierre d'Oléron

Patient are the oyster farmers of Île d'Oléron—they know they must wait four years for each oyster to mature, and during those four years they may well lose fifty percent of their crop. In the 1920s there were forty-eight oyster *cabanes* at Fort Royer, this traditional oyster culture site now preserved and protected by the commune. Today a handful of the oyster shacks remain, all painted with tar to protect them from the weather, and restored to evoke the 1920s.

This is an indoor/outdoor walk-around oyster museum, and you will be especially fortunate if you hook up with well-informed guide Stephanie Guillon.

The Greeks ate oysters with honey, she told us, and sometimes voted with the shells. (There is evidently some debate as to whether the Greeks, Romans, or the Chinese first farmed oysters.) She showed us assorted items on which to encourage little oysters to grow—stones, tiles, slate, lines of shells, iron bars, and today, plastic. We peered into shallow rectangular pools where oysters do their maturing. Once they are two, all snuggled together in packets, they must be cut from the growing material and then separated. Then all the two-year-olds are tossed into a large mesh bag

for their next period of growth. Since an oyster left on its own will grow tall and thin, these bags must periodically be vigorously shaken, to break the edges of the osyters' shells and urge them to become more plump and ovoid.

The tour concludes with a visit to one of the *cabanes,* for a look at tools and gear, and an introduction to one of the oyster's most worrisome natural predators, the armor-piercing winkle. (The acid it releases as it bores into the oyster makes a hole in a jiffy.)

Local oyster tasting was superb at the **Homard Bleu**, a restaurant overlooking the beach at Saint-Trojan-les-Bains, where our tourism office envoy, Frédérique Poisson, did not have to endure even one fish joke. The *langoustines* with *courgettes* were as good as the oysters.

Le Musée des Arts du Cognac, Cognac

Though the salt trade moving up and down the Charente River first gained the town of Cognac its wealth—it was a smooth, direct route to and from the Atlantic Ocean—by the eighteenth century wine had become its key product.

But wine with a difference—merchants from England and the Netherlands, many of them Huguenots with family in Cognac, started to look for ways to ship wine more cheaply, in large quantities, and with less detriment to its quality. The clever solution from the Dutch was *brandewijn,* or burnt wine. (The process also gave birth to an English name for the new drink, brandy.)

The distillation process increased its alcohol content, and decreased its weight by removing the water from the wine. The Dutch didn't think this all up themselves. The Arabs of the Mediterranean had been practicing distillation for medicinal purposes since the eighth century, and Irish monks of the same era seem to have done the same.

The double-distilled blended brandy or *eau de vie* was sealed in oak casks and then put on flat-bottomed river boats called *gabares* uniquely designed to carry the casks

89

The Hôtel Chateau de l'Yeuse in Cognac offers guests 200 different cognacs.

along to the sea, then it was shipped off to northern Europe, where traditionally it was diluted and bottled. But traders liked the taste of the oak-seasoned drink just as it was, and soon stopped that practice. The lure of cognac profits brought English and Irish merchants to France— Richard Hennessey began his distilling business in 1765. By the nineteenth century cognac houses had decided to bottle their brew at home, and so a flurry of ancillary businesses further boosted the local economy.

All this and more is explained at the newly reopened museum.

Aromas and tastes play a major role in determining the perfect blend of a cognac, so the museum designers have

tried to address these elements as well as the more prosaic parts of the story. Cognacs are blended from grapes grown in six different soils or *crus*. Each *cru* may be aged a different length of time, but always in oak barrels. The careful and highly personal blending of these *crus* makes the final product.

The development of bottles, corks, and other packaging as well as marketing materials used in the trade are beautifully displayed. Sound and light shows are part of the mix here as well.

You can also visit assorted exhibitions and displays found at many of the major cognac houses, each a bit different from the other.

At Martel you can view Jean Martel of Jersey's humble cottage—he arrived here from the Channel Islands in 1715. The extensive Hennessey tour carries visitors across the river by boat.

One of the few independent, family-owned-and-run cognac houses is **Camus**, founded in 1863. Here you will very likely run into family members active in the business. They make a point of stressing the personal in their tours.

How personal we had not expected. The night we spent in Cognac, we were invited to have dinner with the Camus

family at their château and became witnesses to an extraordinary tale of a well-traveled bottle of cognac. An American named Quinn Talley was going through his grandfather's things in Washington, DC, after his death. His grandfather's name was B.B. Talley, and he was one of the generals in command of US forces during the D-Day landings in June 1944. On the beach, partially buried in sand, General Talley found a few bottles of cognac, wrapped in straw, each marked in German for the private use of the Nazi officer corps. He carried them home and there they languished in his basement, only one bottle used by his wife from time to time to flavor some cooking. Quinn Talley and his brothers inherited the remaining bottles and Quinn decided to track down their origin—he discovered they had come from a cognac house since bought by Camus, so he contacted Camus in order to arrange the return of one bottle. The night we ate dinner together was the night he handed the historic bottle back to the family, to current president Jean-Paul Camus.

These are three of the many wine museums and displays to choose from in Bordeaux.

Musée des Vins, Bordeaux

Three hundred years of Bordeaux wine history are on display here in the 1720 cellars built by a wine merchant whose biggest client was Louis XV. Also called **Musée des Chartrons** (*chartrons* is another word for wine merchants), this house evidently has been home to a series of merchants, including an Irishman named Duffy.

Vinorama de Bordeaux, Bordeaux

The Madame Tussaud's of wine history, this museum features about seventy-five waxwork figures that take visitors back through time. Its tasting, too, is somewhat different. You can try three Bordeaux wines—one in the Roman style, one from 1850, and one from today. The Romans favored well-aged wines (ten to twenty-five years), high in alcohol content (about fifteen percent), and often added honey and herbs to the mix. So your Roman sample will probably be more like a Madeira than a Bordeaux.

Château Mouton-Rothschild, Pauillac

Not just the history of wine, but the way wine and winemaking has been depicted in paintings and tapestries is the focus of this art collection on the Château's favorite theme. It's a good counterpoint to other wine history exhibits, adding some romance to the mix.

Oh! Légumes Oubliés, Sadirac

Six hundred heirloom edible plants—squashes, artichokes, berries, old local varieties of fruit trees, lettuces, and more—have a home here on a working organic farm dating back to the sixteenth century. Bernard Lafon, the founder, has even revitalized an *Apéritif de Fleur Pissenlit*, or dandelion wine, a farm product people took for granted one hundred years ago. You can taste it. **91**

Southwest:
Aquitaine, Midi-Pyrénées, Limousin

American food writer John Thorne once wrote that the southwest of France, stretching from the Atlantic Ocean east to the Mediterranean, was the land of the "independent-minded goose and pig," those self-sufficient foragers much like the independent people of the former Occitania. Walnuts provided food, furniture, and drink, and goose and duck fat, not butter or olive oil, still smooth the way. The stalwart Occitanians made a regional star of solid, slow-cooked food like *cassoulet*.

Their neighbors the Basques, the oldest and most autonomous people of Europe, had turned their eyes west to the Americas for generations. They were fishing, drying, and salting cod off Newfoundland and Labrador as early as the eleventh century, and selling their products throughout Europe. Basques made up not only the majority of Columbus' crews, they also served as navigators on his voyages, and one of them delivered the chile pepper to Espelette. Another, Juan Sebastien Elkano, the Basque captain who successfully completed Magellan's voyage around the world, first brought America's major native grass, corn, to Spain. By 1563 it had reached Bayonne. Without corn, Bayonne's pigs would not have eaten themselves into the top levels of the ham pantheon. Without the chile pepper, vast numbers of Basque dishes would be relying on some other spice. Even the tomato, another native of the Americas, is a Basque favorite that few of today's dishes could do without. And then there's the most sublime food group from the Americas, chocolate—Biarritz and Bayonne became chocolate centers, thanks to the Jewish community—and chocolate, too, became a Basque favorite.

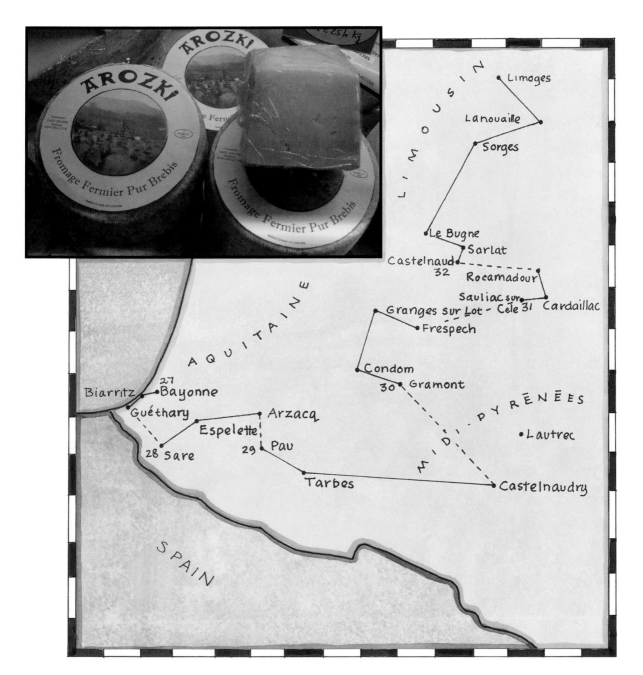

Stage 27: Bayonne to Biarritz to Guéthary

Chocolate, chiles, corn, and more from the Americas; pigs, whales, wheat flour, cherries, and cheese from Eurasia—the Columbian exchange is expressed in all things Basque and beautiful.

Once a museum filled with mannequin-peopled rooms recreating rural life, the new emphasis is on the artifacts and objects themselves, treated much like sculptural art objects.

At the entrance, huge wall-sized changing slides of fishermen, with a men's choir singing in the background, introduce the visitor to Basque country. (A dramatically lighted *chalaud*, or fishing boat carved from one oak tree, is one of the most arresting objects we have seen in a museum.)

The exhibits are in French, Spanish, and Basque. If these languages do not suit, don't worry—the objects are a treat and require little explanation.

Le Musée Basque, Bayonne

Yes, the utterly unexpected rolled bark oboes used by Basque shepherds caught our attention early on, even though food was our main focus. This elegant ethnographic museum about Basque life paints a picture of the "agropastoral" life of the Basque people—beautifully displayed tools and musical gear of shepherds, items used by farmers raising corn, peppers, pigs, and apples, and others processing cider and chocolate. Central to this way of life is the home—a Basque ancestral homestead gives the family its name. Traditionally the "zazulu," or cherry wood, high-backed bench placed near the fire, allowed people to lower a center section, creating an armrest of sorts from which to eat.

94

Not the secret recipe of Madame in charge, but still, a fine way to make your own frothy drink.

Frothy Hot Chocolate

1 serving

Allow about 1 ¼ oz. good quality dark chocolate per cup of milk. Use semi-sweet, or, be a purist and go with unsweetened, adding sugar to taste.

Break up the chocolate into small bits, or shave it into thin strips. Add 1 or 2 tablespoons of milk and melt on low heat. Slowly add the rest of the milk, whisking as you go. Add enough sugar to suit your taste, a tiny pinch of salt, too. Taste. For a drink hearkening back to chocolate's American origins, add a dash of cayenne pepper and whisk away again. (Some have been known to froth this drink up nicely in a blender for about 30 seconds, making sure the lid is on firmly.) Enjoy with thickly sliced, hot buttered toast.

Chocolat Casenave, Bayonne

The waitresses in white-scalloped aprons, long black skirts, low heels, and white blouses are an instant reminder of the English tea shops of yore. As a matter of fact, Bayonne *was* English for about three hundred years, beginning with the marriage of Eleanor of Aquitaine and Henry Plantagenet in the twelfth century.

Yet this is France, the tea is hot chocolate, and there is nothing "yore" about the clientele of all ages and type, drawn here like pilgrims to partake of dark, hot, foamy cocoa (*chocolat mousseux*), thick-cut toast dripping with butter, and tiny dishes of whipped cream that have never known an aerosol can. It's a chocolate shop, one of the oldest here, established in 1845.

You can sit outside under the huge, low arches, or inside, where it's fun to watch the staff thump Feydeau farce-like in and out of the kitchen doors, appearing and reappearing with the same small trays. Okay, here and there an actual cup of tea or coffee is selected, but the fans are here for chocolate. Madame in charge sits at the cashier's desk, impaling tickets on a spindle, making change, and coyly refusing to divulge exactly how the foam on the cocoa cup is achieved. When we asked if we could visit the kitchen she said,

"The *usine* yes, the *cuisine* no"—factory yes, kitchen no.

Musée du Chocolat, Biarritz

That distinct, wickedly enticing chocolate aroma will have your nostrils quivering in the parking lot of the museum. And even as you stand just inside the entrance, learning about the three types of cacao beans grown in the tropics— the original *criollo* cultivated by the Aztecs, and the African *forastero* and Trinidadian *trinitario* derived from it—the odor will draw you deeper into the exhibition. (At the end, after learning all about how chocolate is made, if you're good, you can taste intense cocoa and also sample three different types of chocolate candy.)

This most beneficial and delightful of American natives was brought to Spain sometime after 1524, along with tales of the foamy, warm chocolate drink the Aztecs made with it. Eventually Spanish nobility were drinking spicy mixes of chocolate, vanilla, sugar, cinnamon, and sometimes, chile peppers.

The secret of Spanish chocolate processing came to France with the Jews, who were already involved in cacao trading. Expelled first from Spain and then Portugal, many settled in the Basque capital of Bayonne, and by the mid- to late-seventeenth century were renowned chocolate processors.

Much of the museum is based on the remarkable private collections of Serge Couzigou, a Biarritz chocolate maker. One wall is filled with 3D sample sheets illustrating an enormous range of chocolate molds—these functioned as catalog sheets for prospective chocolate makers. And there are real molds, too, and chocolate pots, invented by the French, with a central hole in which was inserted the whisking device used to foam the cocoa. Mills and roasting machines illustrate the processing of chocolate and chocolate boxes, cocoa tins, even a promotional tandem bike for chocolate company employees, with his-and-her seats— these are all part of a large display of chocolate company promotional items. One early enamel sign from the Delespaul-Havez firm depicts all eight of the family's children, with huge cups of hot chocolate.

Unsurprisingly, there's a shop available, after the tasting, and it offers chocolate products from all the major local firms.

Guéthary whaling site

The Basques were whalers in the seventh and eighth centuries, bringing into European markets the one "red" meat allowed for eating on Fridays by the Catholic Church. By the end of the seventh century, Basque communities all along the Bay of Biscay and on up the Atlantic Coast had erected whale-spotting towers. One in the village of Guéthary is still intact today. Up until early in the twentieth century this small town still had two whaling boats, each crewed by ten men. Recent excavations have revealed a fish-salting factory established here as early as the first century. So make a visit, climb the tower, and then go enjoy a plate of fresh grilled sardines.

Best picnic spot in the area: the cliffs overlooking the long breakers of Bidart's beaches.

Stage 28: Sare to Espelette to Arzacq

Red cherries, red peppers, pink ham.

Le Musée du Gâteau Basque, Sare

If you park at the top of the hill, as we did, you have a lovely hike down into a valley, rich with the sweetest smells of summer, bird song, hens working the steep grassy slopes, and a swift stream. A bucolic environs indeed, and home to a couple of donkeys, a friendly dog, as well as the family behind the museum about Basque country's famous eggy cake.

The old stone and wood building houses the museum, including the teaching area placed in front of a huge fireplace. You can examine a range of baking tools, baskets, and molds but also learn how to bake, as long as you phone ahead to take the class.

Built around lard and corn flour, the traditional recipe used honey as the sweetener. The presence of American corn means the cakes are seventeenth century at the earliest. By the eighteenth century, they were topped with black cherry jam, made from the several cherry varieties that grow well on the Basque coast, and by the end of the nineteenth century custard was another *gâteau*-topping option.

Cherries Were Us, Itxassou

Visit the pretty Basque village of Itxassou the first weekend in June to enjoy its annual **Cherry Festival.** While not the cherry-producing power it once was, Itxassou presents at least three regional varieties of fresh cherries, many processed into an assortment of *confitures*. Local restaurants offer cherry-based dishes and the community puts on Basque dances and *pelote* tournaments.

97

La Fête du Piment, Espelette

All summer until the first frosts of November, chiles dominate the fields of Espelette, where the red-, white-, and green-painted village houses display strings of the drying red pepper from the rafters each autumn. (The only hotel in town, the **Euskadi**, keeps at least a few strings in place year-round.) Juan de Lakotsa, the Basque navigator who accompanied Columbus on his first voyage, may have brought the plant here first. The locals began growing the American native about 1650.

For many years it was only grown as a medicinal plant but luckily for us all, the varieties of Espelette, dried and ground into powder, rapidly became a regional substitute for black pepper. Espelette pepper is at once sweet and just a bit hot—a remarkable combo, in fact, and one we New Mexican visitors found exceedingly attractive.

Since 2000, Espelette pepper products have carried the coveted AOC label. Nine other towns comprise the AOC pepper-growing region, but this small hilltop town has become the chile capital of the area and home base of the producers' association. Year-round the town's shops offer chile tastings and *traiteur* dishes such as *morue aux piments*. But for maximum chile dipping, you might want to time your visit for the last weekend in October. In addition to multiple pepper treats and tastings from street stands, for two days Espelette's **Fête du Piment** overflows with sheep eats: mutton with white beans, sausages with onions, and Brebis cheeses.

Le Piment dans le Monde

The town honors its prized plant with a permanent exposition space on the second floor of the medieval château. The exhibit informally takes you from the pepper's early days in the Americas to its dispersal around the world, mostly through photos and posters, though one section displays actual global chile products. A separate tower room is reserved for photos of the Espelette variety itself.

To taste the AOC product, walk out of the château and left up to the main street—vendors exist all the way along, offering tastings.

Note: Cattle blood, not chile powder pigment, was once used to paint the beams and shutters of Basque houses red.

Piperade

A Basque comfort food found throughout the region, waving the Basque colors of red and green, piperade is a tasty egg dish prepared with tomatoes, peppers, and in this recipe, Bayonne ham.

3 large green peppers
2 large onions, sliced
6 garlic cloves, minced
6 tomatoes, peeled and diced
1 Espelette pepper or pimento cut into rounds,
or, $^1/_4$ t. cayenne powder
4 slices Bayonne ham
8 eggs
olive oil, salt, sugar
chopped parsley for garnish

To easily remove green pepper skins, hold over gas flame or broil in the oven until blackened. Put in a paper bag and let sit for about 10 minutes. You can then easily remove skins with your fingers, take out the seeds, and cut green peppers in $^1/_3$-inch-wide strips.

Cook green peppers, onion, garlic, tomatoes, and Espelette pepper in olive oil slowly for about 30 minutes, with a pinch of sugar, until tomatoes are reduced to a sauce-like consistency. Meanwhile gently heat the ham in a tablespoon of goose fat, if at all possible, or olive oil. Add to the vegetable mix the oil that the ham was warmed in, set slices aside, and keep warm. Beat the eggs and cook quickly on high heat, keeping them moist. Mix together with the pepper/tomato sauce and heat on low for about 2 minutes. Place egg and vegetable mixture on a large warm platter, garnish with parsley, and "crown" with the sliced ham, as the Maison suggests.

Recipe courtesy La Maison du Jambon de Bayonne

Route du Fromage for Brebis cheese

Cheeses made from sheep's milk—*brebis* means ewe—abound along the 200-kilometer **Route du Fromage**. The D 918 starts at the Atlantic Ocean and ends in the foothills of the Pyrénées. You will travel up hill and down dale, stopping for tastings at farmhouses and villages along the way. Ossau-Iraty is the star throughout, a creamy, mountain-meadow AOC choice since 1980 that works as a new cheese or an aged one, and is often served with the regional cherry preserves. The locals call their cheeses "farmers' desserts" but one can start a meal as well as end it with Ossau-Iraty. While relatively new as an AOC, a similar cheese was sold in the markets of Toulouse as early as 1 BC, according to historians.

La Maison du Jambon de Bayonne, Arzacq

Worshipped or reviled, praised as hugely intelligent, condemned as a fan of mud and garbage, in the end the pig is always eaten, often as ham, especially the cured or smoked hind leg of the animal. For over 1,000 years the ham of Bayonne has been particularly prized. The purveyors of this fine, dry-cured product are convinced that their particular microclimate, at the foot of the Pyrénées along the Atlantic coast, bathed in soft winds and humidity, is in large part responsible for their perfect hams. But don't discount the three long days spent rubbing each ham with salt from the Bassin de l'Adour. Nor the long lie-down the hams take on a bed of gray salt for another six months. The last touch before the curing hang? Many Bayonne hams are given a final wipe with the hot yet sweet Espelette dried, ground red pepper.

At the ham museum, even as you are receiving your headsets tuned to a range of languages, you can look down and see such a bed of gray salt under your feet. Look up and you'll observe celestial pigs in a heavenly sky. All things pig are well covered here, starting with a fourteenth-century discovery that the meat of a wild boar downed for some

99

emerges blinking into the light, enticed straight to the tasting area where a fresh dish towel covers a nine- to twelve-month cured Bayonne ham at the ready. The ham some describe as walnut-flavored is served with white wine from *Domaine de Cabidos*, a Pyrénées vineyard.

Additional feature: on request, the museum people will take you outside to their pig barn, to introduce you to the several races of pigs they select to become *jambons de Bayonne*. If you have just finished touring the museum, abuzz with knowledge of the pig's many virtues, including its high intelligence, this visit can be disquieting. The York pig stood up on his trotters to greet us.

time in a salt marsh tasted terrific—perhaps far better than a boar ineptly roasted.

Viewing this exhibition is akin to falling down Alice's rabbit hole, albeit one's passage is all pig—pigs are honored here—in artwork, song, fable, children's books, and poetry. A French family with a pig salted away in a barrel or earthen jug, its hams hanging from the rafters, felt itself well provisioned indeed. Illuminated pig pictures appear in lighted tunnels, above, below, and on each side, and as one enters and leaves an area a new narrative loads in the headphones. A look into a ham drying room, a peek at a slice of ham history, a video on pig and ham processing, and finally, one

100

Stage 29: Pau to Tarbes to Castelnaudry to Lautrec

From tarragon, butter, and egg yolk sauce to today's version of what some think might be an old Arab dish, fava beans and mutton stew.

Brasserie de Berry, Pau

People were lined up outside this neighborhood joint jammed to bursting on a midday Sunday. We scanned many tables as we waited, evaluating the customers' lunches, and knew what we wanted as soon as we were seated. Two trout in butter, please—they came, golden, quivering, served up with salads flopping off the dinner plates, generous sides of *frites*, and a large pot of *sauce Béarnaise* placed center stage on the white paper cloth. The sauce was thick as thieves, mustard yellow, and well-laced with tarragon. We applied it to the bread, the *frites*, the fish, and would have applied it directly to our tongues with the serving spoon had we not maintained a firm grip on our table manners. Lunch for two, with house wine, no dessert, came to twenty Euros.

The Tarbes Beanfields

The white bean raised in Tarbes, a village along the Adour River, became the undisputed bean of choice for *cassoulet* once American native plants began creeping across Europe. The Bishop of Tarbes had spent some time in Spain, enjoying and observing plants brought back from the Americas. In 1712 he introduced to local farmers what the Aztecs called *ayacotl*. Slightly revised as *haricot*, the name stuck in both French and British English. French growers planted the handpicked climbing bean with corn, Native American style, minus the squash. Its heyday was the 1880s—with the advent of intensive farming practices the bean crop dwindled away until local farmers revived the tradition one hundred years later.

By 1996 the buttery bean that holds its shape was granted the Label Rouge as well as IGP status. You can observe up close the production of this labor-intensive, site-specific crop. And celebrate with fellow beaniacs at Tarbes' mid-July Festival.

101

Maison de Cassoulet, Castelnaudry

A slick, modern café done up in shades of chrome, maroon, and mustard, with soul music playing in the background, Olivier Denat's **Maison de Cassoulet** in Castelnaudry does not look like a place starring grandmother's fabled *cassoulet*, a slowcooked, bean-based dish. And yet it is, and it has put its twenty-first-century stamp on an eating tradition that dates back centuries.

Cassoulet itself is a Languedoc specialty named for the red clay pottery from Issel in which it is baked, the *cassole*. Originally made with Europe's only native bean, the fava, since the sixteenth century French cooks have relied on the American native *haricot* bean, in this case a white bean, similar to the Great Northern.

Recipes differ and are fought over in Toulouse, Carcassonne, and Castelnaudry, but the one we tried at Maison de Cassoulet was built from garlic, beans, Toulouse pork sausage, duck *confit*, pork/bacon and carrots, onions, chicken bouillon, and, curiously, one and only one soup-spoon of tomato paste. This melange is baked for anywhere from four to seven hours, and along the way the oily crust is "broken" seven times, according to ancient practice, so as to allow different layers of beans to rise to the surface.

The result? Far more complex and layered than New England baked beans. You can taste distinctly each of the major ingredients and the beans do not become mush, even though cooked so long.

While a few grandmothers and slow food fans still make *cassoulet* at home, Denat says many people today rely on places like his for *cassoulet* for eight to ten people to go. "Yes, France has four major food factories turning out *cassoulet* in cans and jars, using ingredients from all over—many beans are coming from Argentina—but here we try to make the real thing from real French ingredients." There's a move on to acquire AOC status for Castelnaudry *cassoulet*, a dream pushed by the local *Confrerie*, but not yet achieved.

L'Ail Rose (Pink Garlic), Lautrec

In the Middle Ages a peddler low on funds supposedly traded some pink garlic for a meal in Lautrec. The innkeeper planted the bulbs and thus an agricultural specialty was born.

Dip into the annual Garlic Festival put on here the first week in August. The specialty? Garlic soup.

Stage 30: *Gramont to Condom to Granges sur Lot to Frespech*

Explore both the history and modern-day stories of honey, prunes, and *foie gras* at thoughtfully done food museums created by three regional producers.

Musée du Miel, Gramont

50,000 bees and 7,000 visitors each year. Bees have long upstaged people in the lives of Emile and Chantal Moles, proprietors of the ten-year-old honey museum and purveyors of honey products from beeswax to mead, and everything honey in between. The couple does all the bee work themselves, and yes, they do take a vacation, but, in truth says Chantal, "Every vacation is not really a vacation, it's HONEY!" On one trip, with considerable difficulty, they brought back some unique African hives from Morocco.

"Bees have captivated my husband since he was fourteen. And now his passion has become mine as well."

Housed in an old fieldstone farm building, the museum is most proud of its large collection of French hives, from a hollowed-out tree variety—the ancestral homes of wild bees—to a medieval basket hive made from *osier* covered in cow patties, an early wattle and daub technique. The French word *ruche* comes from a word for bark; in the days of Gaul many people carved hives from the cork oak, better to keep the bees warm in winter and cool in summer. The global hive collection includes a Dutch hive woven of straw into the likeness of St Ambrose, a honey-tongued fourth-century bishop who became the patron saint of bees and beekeeping and whose portrait always includes bee imagery.

The museum covers the use of smokers for calming the busy bees in order to grab their honey, knives for removing the combs, presses—some enormous—for extracting the honey, old bee product packaging, and a jam-packed knick-

knack case filled with bee-themed jewelry, toys, honey pots, key chains, and more.

Central to the museum's success with the casual visitor are the five indoor/outdoor Plexiglas hives, including one claimed as the world's largest. In season, from June to September, idle vacationers are riveted on the comings and goings of thousands of hard-working bees.

None work harder than the Moles themselves, who turn out their own brand of honeyed spice cakes and bonbons, in addition to *hydromel* or mead, a beverage the French food historian Maguelonne Toussaint-Samat calls "the ancestor of all fermented drinks," even older than food cultivation itself. This drink created from honey mixed with water had an odd, not altogether pleasant taste that in no way detracted from our appreciation of the miracle of honey and the generosity of its producers.

103

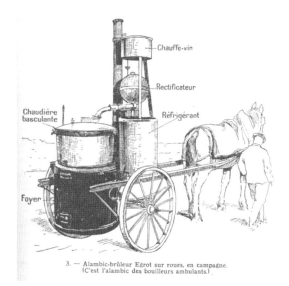

3. — Alambic-brûleur Egrot sur roues, en campagne.
(C'est l'alambic des bouilleurs ambulants.)

Musée de l'Armagnac, Condom

Older than cognac, and probably older than whiskey, Armagnac, unique to the Gascony region, was described in the fifteenth century as a libation that "gives vivacity to the mind, and cheerfulness." By the seventeenth century distilled products were big business, as unlike wine, they did not deteriorate in transit and they were happily higher in alcohol content. More gusto for the guilder, as the Dutch were the biggest traders in distilled spirits.

The museum depicts all the stages involved in creating the rough and ready Armagnac, from plucking the white grapes, to pressing them—they display the world's largest wine press—to distilling them in the large collection of alambics gathered here. The extensive collection was first assembled in the 1950s and includes a huge array of tools, baskets, glasses, barrels, and bottles.

Musée du Pruneau, Granges sur Lot

While the California prune marketers are vigorously trying to convert us from saying "prunes" to saying "dried plums," in France a "prune" is still a plum and a *"pruneau"* is a

prune. And prunes here in the Agen region are sublime, nothing like the slimy ones some of you may remember being doled out once a week at school and summer camp. Most all the plums grown here descend from plants originating in Asia—it seems at least four strains combined over two thousand years ago to produce one variety—with folklore insisting that the Damson plum, originally from Damascus, Syria, was brought to France by returning Crusaders. Yet food historians think that variety already was in Roman hands by the first century.

Jean-Louis Martinet, born in Algeria, returned with his family at the age of ten to their ancestral home and to the plum growing and drying business. In the 1980s he became seriously curious about the history of the process in his region of Granges sur Lot and began collecting the ovens and associated baskets that made it all possible.

His museum, set in a warehouse attached to his business, begins with a huge collection of oxen yokes from all over the world, his collecting passion before prune memorabilia. But the prune story begins with ovens. In the old days before commercial prune production, people would take their plums to the bakery to be dried. Since the ovens of the region were round, the locals made graceful teardrop or leaf-shaped baskets to hold the plums, so that several of them could fit together in a circle. The shape continued long after the round ovens were a memory. (Early prune ovens also served as dryers for the linens that were part of every family's household.)

The museum displays many such early wood-fired ovens, but also the tools, packaging, and memorabilia associated with the business. A curious US-French prune connection crops up in the exhibit. In December 1856 a man named Pierre Pellier left Agen for California, intent on joining his brother Louis there and making his fortune in Gold Rush times.

He carried with him two trunks, each filled with plum cuttings from Agen set in potatoes. The clever M. Pellier assumed the moist potatoes would keep the tiny plants hydrated. Surviving the journey, these plants were grafted onto wild American plums to produce today's California

Prune, oops, Dried Plum. Later in the Franco-American plum relationship, American engineers took a look at French drying ovens, greatly improved them, and now many such ovens used in France are either of American origin or incorporate American-conceived improvements.

Next to the sales and tasting room you can watch a video with English and German subtitles about how plums are turned into prunes. And in late summer you can wander through the operation's other foodie tourist offering, a maize maze.

On the way to the Prune Museum, spur of the minute, we pulled into **Longuesserre & Fils**, growers and processors of *pruneaux d'Agen*. There we were warmly greeted by Anne-Marie Longuesserre, the retired daughter of the founder. She showed us the drying ovens; the factory where employees turn out prunes dipped in chocolate, among other treats; the entire product line; and a photo of her father, Roger, aged two, in 1906, "helping" two elderly ladies sort prunes.

Musée de Foie Gras, Frespech

Three kilometers from the tiny town of Frespech in what the locals still call Occitania, *foie gras* producers Yves and Genevieve Boissière have created an imaginative museum about their region's most famous product. Though Alsace was the beginning of *foie gras* fame, today eighty percent of French *foie gras* comes from the southwest.

Wild geese started off the craze for "fat liver" and its succulent derivatives. People observed that the geese ate heartily before beginning their long migratory flights—those that were killed had plump, delicious livers. So over 4,000 years ago the Egyptians began force-feeding captive geese with balls of grain, largely millet. The Romans tried feeding them figs, liked the result, and inadvertently created the Italian word for liver, *fegato*, derived from fig.

Up until the 1950s in France domesticated geese, gulping down fifty pounds of grain in their final three weeks, were the norm. Today, ducks rule in *foie gras* production—they are less expensive, easier to handle—and the turnaround is faster on these corn mash-fed fowl.

Boissière and his wife converted his grandfather's dairy barn into the museum in 1994 because visitors to the farm kept asking so many questions. The four major exhibit areas—history, breeding, cooking, and marketing—address many of these questions and offer up offbeat tidbits.

Goose feathers were used to clean chimneys, and turkeys were enticed with saucers of *eau de vie*, clear fruit brandy, so they would sit on nests of up to twelve goose eggs. Geese, for no apparent reason, were poor "sitters." Tipsy turkeys evidently filled the bill.

The worrisome practice of *gavage*, the force-feeding of the birds through funnels inserted in the throat, is displayed, and the proprietor underscores the fact that everything on his farm is done with respect and kindness towards the ducks.

A video explains the entire *foie gras* process and includes footage of the family's amiable dog gently herding ducks. Duck fat, happily, is good for you—the Occitanians swear by it as a booster of good cholesterol—and the house specialties here are exquisitely tasty. *Magret de canard*, boneless duck breast, with *foie gras*, accompanied by a sweet local wine, and traditional *foie gras* laced with yellow fat, had us purring nicely.

Information available in French, English, and Occitan.

Taulejada, the restaurant created by the Boissières from Frespech's fourteenth-century ramparts, features products from the farm. Open July and August for lunch and dinner.

Stage 31: Sauliac sur Cele to Cabrerets to Rocamadour

Go caving to see the raw ingredients of prehistoric peoples' food dreams, then compare two farm museums

Cuzels Musée de Plein Air du Quercy, Sauliac sur Cele, Lot

This is the Fibber McGee's closet of open-air museums, several gently rolling acres of land overflowing with cultural and agricultural curiosities, including two museums within the museum—one all about fire and electricity—lighting, cooking, burning at the stake!—the other about the history of water and water *cachement*. If you enjoy the eclectic and offbeat in the world of food history, this is for you. The medieval farmhouse, with its small waste water hole, illuminated the true meaning of "it's just a hole in the wall." The same building, dark, cramped, and uncomfortable, had a black-singed open hearth. Its adjacent precursor to a barn was a wood A-frame, open on one end, and stuffed with rye grasses. Still, by the 1800s Quercy farms were prosperous and thriving right up until the decline of the vineyards caused by *phylloxera*.

Stroll in and out of chicken coops and outbuildings—the grange is one of the largest in France—to learn about stone cutting, view a coffee pot collection, compare assorted water-carrying devices, including an elegant copper pot

interpreted from differing perspectives, the twentieth century and the twenty-first.

women placed on a ring of straw perched on their heads. Dip into strawberry, fig, and wine culture, basket making, yokes and gear for horses, old trucks and tractors, tools of every variety, even bikes, a slew of them, rusting *en plein air*.

In summer visitors can observe milling and bread making, and chat with potters, stone cutters, and barrel makers. (Parisian school children on their *vacances scolaire* were delighted to show us the wooden *sabots* they had just made in the workshop at the museum.) On special theme days you can taste local honeys, wines, cheeses, saffron, duck products, and more.

Any day, you can stroll right up to the front steps of the odd central building, a château built in 1930 whose top floor burned away twenty years later.

Last restored in 1985, badly needing a facelift and a tidying, the Quercy Museum still has its considerable charms.

Pech-Merle Cave, Cabrerets

While prehistoric people were surviving primarily on berries, grubs, nuts, small mammals, fish, tubers, and bits of grain, they were ever hopeful of landing the big one, enough meat for a clan party, with leftovers. Their 25,000-year-old cave paintings immortalize the woolly mammoths, bison, and aurochs so difficult to bring down, rather than the more humdrum ingredients of their everyday larders. Of course this is a foodie take on the drawings—probably not the typical anthropological view.

As we descended into the cave of Pech-Merle in the Dordogne, we were with a select party of cave groupies, amateur experts who had visited caves in many parts of the globe. We quickly caught on that the current view is not to laud the drawings as "art" but to explore how and when they were **107** made. To point out, for example, how expertly their creators made use of the rock's existing features, bringing the animals to the surface much as Michelangelo freed his *prigioni* from the marble. But when we saw the red outline of a fine-looking fish, thought to be a pike, we couldn't help but wonder if it would have been grilled or smoked. Or maybe even poached, possibly eaten with a bit of lamb's ear salad...

Musée Eclaté, Cardaillac

An actual village as museum, Cardaillac invites visitors to pop into the barrel-maker's house, visit the walnut oil mill, view the chestnut-drying ovens, and more. This fieldstone village boasting a twelfth-century tower was in the thick of the religious wars, as one of the most populous Protestant communities in Quercy.

La Borie d'Imbert, Rocamadour

Just along a winding country road northwest of the twelfth-century cliffside town of Rocamadour is a new style of high-tech theatrical museum attraction, a living farm where the visitor is inserted back in time. The farmhouse was built in 1825, then added onto in 1858. The forty acres of Quercy limestone earth on which it sits date back to the twelfth century when Cistercian monks held the land—as the director and our guide put it, "the peasants helped the monks and the monks developed the agricultural practices."

The museum picks up the history of the place, known as Justine's Farm, just after the Great War. When you step inside the farmhouse, you are invited to sit on a bench. The light dims and before you the soup pot on the fire gets red, then steams. Then you hear the voice of Justine's son Paul, killed in the war, as he speaks longingly of home. This *animation* of light and sound succeeds admirably at both informing and moving the visitor, as the little house tells its stories. Justine and her husband lost two sons in battle, and two babies in infancy. Now they live alone.

The light jumps from the walnut oil lamps, to the olive wood rosary, to the shell casing made into a decorative object.

The show ends and the guided tour begins in the bedroom, under which was the *cave*, as was typical in this region—the giant grape-pressing vats used by Justine and her husband are still there, visible through a Plexiglas window, once a trapdoor. Stories are told of the carbon dioxide rising from the crushed grapes, which gave people terrible headaches. Our guide relates that men often spent a lot of time down below, to escape the women gathered in the kitchen.

Justine kept a few chickens, goats, some ducks, a pig or two, and a donkey, as well as a kitchen garden. The garden is planted in old varieties—including salsify and saffron. There is one elderly grapevine left, said to be a hearty survivor in the Justine mode, untouched by the *phylloxera* attack that had destroyed almost two-thirds of continental Europe's vineyards by the close of the nineteenth century.

On July 4, 2004, the farm inaugurated its first Saffron Festival, honoring the plant that was a Quercy tradition between the fifteenth and seventeenth centuries. Today local farmers are once again planting the crocus bulbs from which saffron is harvested.

Cross the street and you can view the lovely brown-faced goats of the Chevrerie and then tour the Fromagerie, finishing by tasting the fruits of their labors, the tangy AOC Rocamadour cheese.

Stage 32: Castelnaud to Sarlat to Le Bugne to Sorges to Lanouaille to Limoges

From walnuts to geese, from truffles to apples, then offal.

Ecomusée de la Noix du Perigord, Castelnaud-la-Chapelle

Noix may translate into English as "nuts," but in France all *noix* are walnuts.

The French have been cracking *noix* since Neolithic times—archaeologists have found petrified walnut shells in the Périgord—and actively cooking and baking with them since about the fourth century. Walnut oil is many locals' favorite for salads, as indeed it was for René of Anjou. A fifteenth-century Neapolitan and King of Sicily, René disliked the ubiquitous olive oil of Provence so much that he arranged for the planting of scores of Périgord walnut trees in Aix, the Provençal town in which he died.

A lawyer who lives in Bordeaux bought this old *noyeraie* of about 260 trees, complete with mill and outbuildings. He restored it all, installed his parents there for their retirement years, and soon, before his mother could bolt for the nearest *Troisième Age* facility, she found herself running her son's elegant museum of the walnut.

A video on modern walnut growing and processing can either begin or end your tour, on two floors of the old grange. White plaster walnuts, lifesize as well as outsized, are used throughout, either as signposts or background to the well-researched displays. The museum features a cartoon-style running commentary on history, botany, and so on, in the form of multi-lingual flip charts in each area. Noteworthy items? A nude carved from the root of an ancient walnut, and the walnut oil lamps once used in the village hanging near the walnut press, running in season at the museum.

In the shop you can sample oil, walnut cakes, and walnut liqueurs, all products that remind us of the influence and importance of walnuts on this region. A local crafts person sells one-of-a-kind wooden nut crackers, of the local mallet-and-bowl type, as well. The owner has provided ample parking and picnic areas, and a well-marked (those giant white plaster walnuts again) stroll through the nuttery.

A cartoon history of the walnut and info on its growing and processing is available in French, Spanish, German, and English.

Place du Marché-aux-Oies, Sarlat la Caneda

Pet the goose statue, and on autumn and winter Saturdays, linger in the live goose portion of Sarlat's market. You might also take a gander at this town's impeccable thirteenth-century medieval streets and buildings.

Musée Vivant de l'Oie—Collonges la Rouge

At the **Ferme de Veyries** you can get up-close and personal with live geese, of assorted varieties, some stemming from Australia and Hungary, and also visit a grange exhibition about goose history—from feathers to *gavage*.

109

Ecomusée de la Truffe, Sorges

France consumes more black truffles than any other country (white truffles are found in Italy's Piedmont region), eating all of its own forty-ton-plus production per year, importing another forty from Italy and Spain, and over twenty tons from China as well. And we're talking fungi of the genus *Tuber Melanosporum*, resembling knobbly brown golf balls, which grow among the roots of infected oak trees, three to twelve inches underground.

Appetizing? Evidently. This culinary oddity with the complex musky aroma and the just-unearthed-by-the-pig's-snout taste is so prized people may well pay more for this per pound, $500 to $600, than for any other food.

France's truffle heyday began with the *phylloxera* attack on wine stocks about 1880, when vineyard owners desperate for an alternative crop went with the oak tree/truffle combo. In the south and southwest of France "black diamonds" became such big business that local farmers were soon roofing their homes with slate, a sure sign of financial solvency. World War I of course changed all that, wiping out much of the young male population. *Truffières* went untended, and as years passed intensive farming techniques suitable for grain growing did further damage to the production of truffles.

The revitalization of the industry began about twenty years ago.

Famous for its truffles in the early twentieth century, the village of Sorges in Périgord hosts the **Museum of the Truffle**, in a restored fieldstone building you can't miss because the world's largest sculpted truffle hangs from one end of it. Each year about 8,000 visitors explore the Truffle Association's extensive exhibition and then stroll among the three kilometers of *truffières*, truffle orchards strewn with pale, potato-like, limestone chips.

While the exhibit's information is mostly conveyed through static posters, flat art, and photos, no facet of truffle history and production is overlooked. The tiny shop at the entrance sells a range of truffle books, some in English, and, in tiny processed quantities, the truffles themselves. Don't miss the finely done plaster repros of truffles, for sale as well. Dominique Delage, the museum's director, is usually on hand and extremely generous about answering questions.

Le Musée de la Boucherie, Limoges

A turn-of-the-nineteenth-century butcher shop, in a building designated for butchery over the past seven hundred years, welcomes visitors fittingly on rue de la Boucherie. Here you can revisit the good old days when carcasses hung bleeding into the sawdust just beyond the customers' eyes, and see how the butcher and his family lived and worked.

Every year during the first week in October the butchers of Limoges set up shop outside on the rue de la Boucherie for their **Frairie des Petits Ventres**, offering customers choice meats, tastes of *les petits ventres*, or tripe, and other delectations. The day-long fair dates back to the year 930.

Maison de La Pomme d'Or, Lanouaille

Sir Isaac Newton is sitting on a bench to welcome visitors to this all-apple exhibition, and William Tell and Snow White make appearances as well.

The Gauls had the apple long before the Romans invaded with their own, possibly better varieties, a collision that certainly improved things for apple lovers in France.

The apple's botanical and mythological story is told here, the apple in art is well represented, and apple growers, too, have their labors explained.

This celebration of the apple also includes this crowning glory: on October 22, 2000 people of this community created the world's largest apple tart, from 14,400 apples. The tart measured fifteen meters, twenty in diameter. How it was baked is unclear...but the Maison claims everything is on file with the *Guinness Book of World Records*.

(The North Central Washington Museum in the US supposedly baked a fifteen-ton apple pie back in 1997 that still seems to be on record with Guinness, too, but a pie is not necessarily a French tart.)

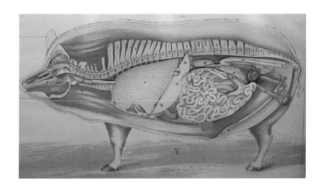

Center West:
Centre, Pays de la Loire, Île de France, Paris

The garden of France.

Here in the western side of the heart of France, where the rolling plains of Limousin flow out of the Dordogne and into the fertile Loire valley, a significant food revolution occurred. In 1533, fourteen-year-old Tuscan Catherine de Medici came to be married to another fourteen-year-old, the future Henri II. Lonely and out of place, Catherine found solace in the foods of her Italian homeland, many of them vegetables not familiar to the French. The chefs she brought with her introduced artichokes and melons, broccoli, peas, green beans, and guinea hens. It is also claimed that her chefs steered the French kitchen staff away from slabs of meat rubbed with spices in the medieval style to a more subtle way of cooking with flavored sauces.

Other subtleties? The fork, and delicious desserts like zabaglione and sorbets.

Later in life, after Henry died, Catherine tossed his life-long mistress Diane de Poitiers from the Loire château, Chenonceau, and installed both herself and a fine garden there.

Today the Loire area still features extraordinary vegetable gardens, and the heart of France continues to produce all manner of fruits, vegetables, grains, and meats.

The region also offers unusual accommodation—we actually lodged as a Loire mushroom might, or, perhaps better, as a fine bottle of wine at rest.

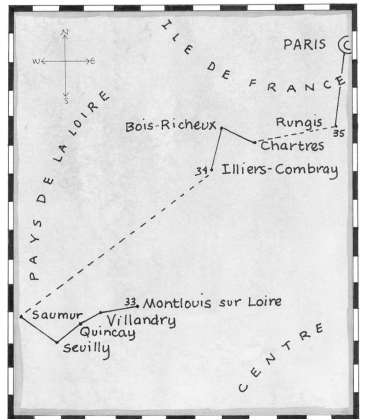

Made from partridge or duck mixed with foie gras and spices, pâte de Chartres *has been a city speciality for over 300 years.*

We became troglodytes for the night and stayed in a cave at the **B&B run by Cathy and Alain Sarrazin in Azay-le-Rideau**.

Once the carved-from-*tuffeau* home of the original farmer and his family, the troglodyte room is now a voluptuous, blazing white nest with more curves than the Loire. (*Tuffeau* is the luminous building material of the graceful châteaus perched on or above the Loire. It was also used by lesser mortals for their houses. Only the poorest people moved into the caves left by the extraction of stone. Locals dubbed them "troglodytes," after the wrens that build nests in small holes.)

The bed perches on a platform, next to a tiny room containing the tiniest tub on earth. From bed you can gaze down into the two-way fireplace, sparking with a warm fire at our arrival. Down a couple steps from the bed ledge, there's a full kitchen and a living area. The Sarrazins supply a sound system and CDs, too, and presumably a TV, though the fire proved captivating enough. Breakfast is eaten family style just outside the cave room door, where the farmer used to house his animals

113

Stage 33: Montlouis sur Loire to Villandry to Quincay to Saumur

A cornucopia of veggies, goat edibles from a cheery hostelry, and offerings from the caves.

Château de la Bourdaisière, Montlouis sur Loire

Five hundred tomato varieties comprise the extraordinary historical collection maintained here by Prince Louis Albert de Broglie, who owns this fifteenth-century château with his brother Philippe Maurice. Louis Albert is the tomato prince—he evidently asked a *Herald Tribune* journalist, "With 10,000 varieties of tomatoes, why should they all be round and red with no taste?"

First planted in Europe, probably Italy, in the mid-sixteenth century, the original tomato was small, gold, and pear-shaped, hence its Italian name, *pomo d'oro*. After the South American natives, the Italians were the primary propagators of the tomato, a fruit, and, like the potato, a relative of deadly nightshade. Because of this horticultural relationship, for a long time many people thought the tomato was toxic, and preferred to enjoy it as an ornamental.

Luckily for us all, that has changed. Late August is the best time to tour this garden, utterly dedicated to an American native, and even to spend the night and eat tomato specialties.

Château Villandry

Finished about 1536 on the banks of the Loire, this glorious château especially appeals to us for what's outside, not inside. Its 12,000-square-meter *potager* or kitchen garden, formally divided into nine different beds, is a veggie's dream—giant cabbages, ornamentals and edibles, pumpkins, radishes, lettuces, artichokes, eggplant, strawberries, leeks, tomatoes, and more, all edged with annual flowers. Running parallel to it and close to the Château's church is the herb garden.

All the plants are selected first for their beauty and design, but any chef would be happy to cook and eat what's growing here.

The first weekend in September you can talk with the kitchen gardeners, and buy produce directly from the Château.

L'Etape Gourmande, Villandry

We were almost forty minutes late arriving at this enticing goat farm and inn, racing to keep on schedule, and we were truly hungry. Madame Beatrice de Montferrier greeted us as calmly and warmly as if we were old friends just running a bit late. And in a wink, our table had been served with *terrine* of goat prepared with port and shallots, as well as *foie gras*. Madame regretted that it was not quite the season for cooked goat so instead she offered guinea fowl served with bacon, spinach, and wild mushrooms and quail, served with endive and mint.

And for dessert, there was plenty of goat cheese ice cream with pistachio nougat biscuits.

The de Montferriers arrived here in this seventeenth-century setting in 1980, after living several years in Mexico, and began raising goats, then making cheese, and finally, when a friend asked if she could eat something under their mulberry trees, started a restaurant and small inn on the premises. Everything they serve is grown either by them or locally and all is organic and fresh. You can visit with the goats, spend the night, and sit under the mulberry trees that started it all.

La Poire Tapée à l'Ancienne, Quincay

Blanched, dried, tapped, and then preserved in wine, in cider, or in *eau de vie*, these pears are delicious. They—or rather, their processing—are the last of a dying breed. Revived by two out-of-work folks in 1995, the old method of oven-drying and preserving pears is working well for Christine and Yves Herin. For generations Loire Valley farmers grew and then preserved fruit by drying them in wood-fired ovens set in the *tuffeau* or limestone caves carved from the hillsides along the river. They then shipped their products up and down the river in square sailboats called *gabares*.

These days the sixty ovens once operating in this area are down to three, and these are fired up each autumn at La

Poire Tapée. (The Herins' cave came with a two-hundred-year-old oven, and they subsequently added two more of newer vintage.) As many as eight different varieties of pears are dried on racks for about 120 hours, on each side. Then one by one, the pears are gently tapped or tamped down with a wooden press reminiscent of a nut cracker. This allows the final breakdown of cells and the elimination of air pockets prior to either being packed in cellophane or placed in jars.

Christine Herin holds a traditional wooden device used to press air out of pears.

The Poire William of *eau de vie* fame is the same pear as the familiar American Bartlett, and in either red or yellow, the most frequently used pear here, with the General leClerc and the Colmar more genuinely French favorites.

The busy Herins welcome visitors to their troglodyte caves every day, showing off old tools and *poire tapée* artwork, explaining the old ways of the wood-fired ovens, creating their impressive range of products, and yes, offering some tastings. While entry to the cave is free, a tasting costs at this writing two Euros. *Poires tapées* products created in the old manner are not inexpensive.

115

Musée du Champignon, Saumur

Louis XIV's gardeners are said to have cultivated mushrooms at Versailles, but more probably in nearby caves; the white mushrooms, raised on aged horse manure, *Agaricus campestris,* were soon dubbed "champignons de Paris." France became the first leading commercial grower of fungi. These days mushroom growers deliver us shitake, maitake, oyster, and more, and people still collect wild field mushrooms all over the world.

Forgive us if we mention first that on a blustery cold day—after walking through the many underground rooms of the always chilly museum, ducking for the low stone ceilings, and navigating the rough earthen floors—the hot mushroom soup, served near a warm fire in the cave's tasting area, was superb.

The museum inhabits multiple rooms in a cave that once raised many tons of mushrooms for sale. These days the staff raises a ton of mushrooms a month in order to reveal the fungi's mystery to visitors. The tour starts with a look at some of the more than 1,800 edible mushroom varieties—some of these are in vials, some reproduced in plastic. This area informs indeed. But the sight of button mushrooms poking up through the growing medium in huge

plastic bags, of the exotics clinging like colorful bats to a pressed-sawdust growing medium, hanging in long cylinders from the ceiling, stimulates an appetite not only for tasting but also for trying to grow these delicacies at home.

Back above ground in the tasting room, you can explore the personal collection of the museum's owner, a self-described mushroom maniac: cufflinks, pins, salt and pepper sets, magnets, candles, blown-glass pieces, Russian Christmas ornaments, all mushroom in shape or scope.

Intérieur d'une carrière à champignons - XIXème siècle

Stage 34: Seuilly to Illiers-Combray to Bois Richeux to Chartres

Food for thought from literary diners, a food list from Charlemagne, and the bounty of wheat offerings are capped by the artful farming machines that made it all possible.

La Devinière, Seuilly

Purportedly the birthplace of François Rabelais, the author of the five-volume *La Vie de Gargantua et de Pantagruel*. Evidently it isn't quite his birthplace, as he emerged while his mother was en route from Chinon to the family's country house in Seuilly. Close enough.

The man whose lusty, coarse, food- and drink-loving characters led to the coining of the word "rabelaisian" was a doctor, teacher, and priest (1494–1553).

La Maison de Tante Léonie – Musée Marcel Proust, Illiers-Combray

"The taste was that of the little piece of madeleine which on Sunday mornings at Combray (because on those mornings I did not go out before mass), when I went to say good morning to her in her bedroom, my aunt Léonie used to give me, dipping it first in her own cup of tea or tisane."

Remembrance of Things Past

A holy site for some, this is the place of the *madeleine* moment, the house visited by the young Marcel Proust during summers as a boy. He was six when he first came to stay with his paternal uncle and aunt, Jules and Elisabeth Amiot, and by the time he was nine the visits ended—his family decided his asthma worsened here. We learned from the ticket taker who sits behind a huge table of Proustiana at the entry that Auntie never baked *madeleines* herself—she always bought them from the bakery around the corner, still there today.

You can visit this charming house and garden or simply peek in through the gates and then trot up the street to buy *madeleines*.

La Ferme Médiévale de Bois Richeux

An active farm since the Celts lived in the Chartres region over 2,000 years ago, by the twelfth century Bois Richeux was one of the first domains to be worked by free peasants, not serfs. Throughout the Middle Ages it was a fortified enclave, with a manor house, chapel, barn, and capacious pigeon house. Today the gardens are maintained according to garden plans of the twelfth century—a medicinal herb plot, an aromatic plot, and a kitchen garden, the latter containing the edible plants listed in Charlemagne's famous proscribed mandate for just about everything, issued in 812. From almonds to walnuts, apples to turnips, Charlemagne had it covered in his *Capitulare de Villes*.

The owners of this private estate surrounded by wheat fields welcome visitors, stressing the spiritual quality of their gardens and hinting at the presence of ancient ghosts hiding just out of sight.

Chartres

Just as Chartres cathedral is surrounded by wheat fields, so too is Chartres' famous filling pâté encased in a wheat crust. Leaving the ancient farm in Bois Richeux, you can still approach the cathedral from the northwest as villagers of the Middle Ages riding or walking to town must have done, and see its spires rising up from the wide golden plain. This is the heart of France's wheat production, the bread basket of France, so again, it's not surprising to discover a wheat beer, Bière de Chartres, promoting itself as "the beer of the Yellow Guard from wheat of Beauce."

Beauce just initiated a *Route de Blé*, or **Wheat Route**, and associated events, including a **wheat beer festival** in the village of Ouarville, at its windmill.

Any and all Chartres specialties, including the pâté, is available at **Le Grand Monarque**, a hotel that has been a roadside attraction since the fifteenth century, when it was a "relais" inn, or relay stop for the delivery of mail. In those days the distance between stops was about 28 km, the "seven leagues" appellation attached to the coachman's boots. Many inns across France still retain the description *relais*, a place where good food and drink were available at all hours.

But beyond its centuries-old traditions the hotel has a unique food history section of its own—take a look at the exhibition of antique toy and sample stoves displayed high up on one wall of the **Restaurant Georges**.

COMPA, Chartres

A handsomely renovated old locomotive repair barn today houses the **Conservatoire de l'Agriculture**, a museum about agriculture built around a collection of 1,200 tools and machines dating from 1800 to the 1950s. Strolling through farm machinery is not for everyone, but these pieces have been so beautifully restored the experience is akin to walking through a sculpture garden. And COMPA has superb temporary exhibits in partnership with other museums. For example, we saw an exhibition all about milk, butter making, and so on, done with the **Musée de Bretagne**, Rennes, and featuring fine antique pieces from their collections.

Stage 35: Rungis to Paris to Saint Denis to Aulnay

Paris should be crowned a living food heritage site, a monument to feeding an urban population, though it has no definite food museums. (Our focus for this book is on France as a whole—tracking down historic sites and foodie shrines of Paris is for another day.) As most foodie travelers would agree, its claim to being the birthplace of the modern restaurant is enough.

A city dating back 2,000 years, Paris has been feeding people since its beginnings as a fishing village on an island in the middle of a river that became the Seine. In fact **Les Halles**, the legendary sprawling Paris food market that is no more, began in 1110 with a few fish stalls set up outside Louis VI's palace. By 1137 evidently it was the world's largest market. Its official modern-day site took ten years to build and was completed in 1866. (In 1873 Emile Zola wrote a novel centered on Les Halles called Le Ventre de Paris, or The Belly of Paris.)

Torn down in 1969 and moved to Rungis, today the market claims again to be the world's largest wholesale fresh product enterprise, employing over 12,000 people in more than 1,300 businesses, including twenty-three restaurants. While you can no longer hang out amidst the hustle-bustle, slightly seamy, all-night people parade that

was Les Halles, slurping onion soup directly across from the onion buyers and sellers, you can arrange group tours of Rungis during daylight hours.

In order to have markets—and Paris has long been a city of markets—food had to be produced and brought into Paris by an army of gardeners, farmers, processors, and teamsters who lived and worked on the edges of the urban area. A museum in Saint Denis, **Le Musée des Cultures Legumières** or **Ecomusée de la Courneuve** on the way to Charles DeGaulle Airport, is dedicated to the traditions and folkways of these ancient professions vital to Parisian food heritage, though closed for reorganization at the time of the research for this book.

First there were markets, and then, increasingly, hungry traders and travelers. The Chinese are said to have had restaurants from the twelfth century, but the French coined the word and probably too created the modern edition of a place in which to sit down, choose your food, and eat, away from home.

In the early days travelers either bought meals from street vendors or supped at overnight inns where they slept. The French tradition of *table d'hote* began here, eating whatever and whenever the innkeeper and his family ate. *Traiteurs*, now the source of superb prepared food for busy working people, operated more like the caterers of today.

But a *restaurant* originally was a restorative, highly condensed meat broth that was taken in small cups, often at a *restaurateur*. Since a good deal of meat went into these tiny cups, they were an indulgence mostly enjoyed by the rich.

Eventually, after the Revolution, lesser mortals began gathering to eat actual dishes, chosen from a menu, in rooms separate from the kitchen. They paid only for what they ate, and by 1820 the restaurant closely resembled what we know today. And for decades Paris was really the only city in France to have restaurants. (For more see *The Invention of the Restaurant* by English historian Rebecca Spang.)

You can try out some Paris eateries that claim to be the oldest in town (many vie for this honor). Paris's oldest house, the 1407 **Auberge Nicholas Flamel**, was the home of the Flamel family who regularly offered food to the poor. It's at 51, rue de Montmorency Paris 3°. The oldest café may be the 1686 **Restaurant Le Procope** at 13, rue de l'Ancienne-Comédie. Voltaire's table is still there, the famous revolutionaries Marat and Danton mixed caffeine and politics

there, and Victor Hugo loved it, but then, he ate around. The oldest *brasserie*? **Le Polidor**, 41 rue Monsieur-le-Prince, said to be a favorite spot of Paul Valery and James Joyce.

One individual getting long-overdue recognition for turning a restaurant into a restaurant is **Mathurin Roze de Chantoiseau**, who began his business in 1766. Among the first to advertise his place on rue Saint Honore as a modern restaurant, he also devised a directory of businesses, including places to eat, and rated them (his efforts were much copied elsewhere). His hometown of Chantoiseau, a village near Fontainbleau Palace, should certainly serve as one of our foodie shrines. Had he lived into the nineteenth century he would probably have promoted Gustave Eiffel's wild and crazy tower restaurant, the first in the world, at the Eiffel Tower.

On the way back to De Gaulle, after our six-and-a-half-week Tour de France, we stopped to get airplane provisions in **Aulnay sur Bois**, a multi-ethnic, busy suburban commuter spot. Near the main train station across from the covered market was a line-out-the-door *traiteur*. Here we waited our turn, surveying all the remarkable cheeses, meats, and prepared dishes that were a veritable gustatory review of our trip. We witnessed how each customer was carefully and patiently tended to, and enjoyed experiencing, one last time, the care, quality, and beauty that is so typical of the continuing food heritage of France.

Information

Travelers should be advised that opening hours, telephone mumbers and web addresses do change.
Please check with local tourism offices for the most up-to-date information.

Center East

Maison-Atelier, J.F. Millet, Barbizon
27, rue Grande
Admission free
Hours: Open every day, 9:30–12:30 and
14:30–17:30 except for Sunday and Tuesday.
Tel: 01 60 66 21 55. Call ahead for groups
as space is tight.

Musée du Safran, Boynes
www.coeur-de-france.com/safran.html
Hours: April 1–November 1: Saturday,
Sunday, and Holidays, 14:30–18:00
Groups by Appointment
Tel: Office du Tourisme de Pithiviers, 02 38
30 50 02; or M. Templier, 02 38 33 13 05.

La Coutellerie de Laguiole, Thiers
Route d'Aubrac, Zone Artisanale La
Poujade, Laguiole
Hours for the museum: July and August,
every day, 9:00–12:00 and 14:00–18:00.
Hours for the studio tour: Monday–Friday,
guided tours at 11:00, 14:30, 15:45 and 17:00.
Tel: 05 65 51 23 47

**Maison de la Gentiane, Riom es
Montagnes**
1 avenue Fernand Brun
Hours: July and August, open every day,
10:00–12:30 and 14:30–17:30
Tel: 04 71 78 10 45

**Musée de l' Agriculture d'Auvergne—
L'Ostal de le Marissou, Coltines**
www.coltines.com/musee1.htm
Tel: 04 71 73 27 30

**Société Roquefort, Roquefort
Fromageries Papillon**
Tel: 05 65 58 50 08 or
Société Roquefort
Avenue de Lauras, Roquefort
Hours: July and August, 9:30–18:30.
Tel: 05 65 59 93 90

Southeast

Musée de l'Etang de Thau, Bouzigues
Hours: July–August, 10:00–12:30 and
14:30–19:00; November–Februrary,
10:00–12:00 and 14:00–17:00; March–June,
September–October: 10:00–12:00 and
14:00–18:00.
Tel: 04 67 78 33 57

Agropolis, Montpellier
www.museum.agropolis.fr
Hours: Open every day except Tuesday,
14:00-18:00.
Tel: 04 67 04 75 00

Musée du Bonbon Haribo, Uzes
Hours: Closed the first three weeks in
January. Call for hours.
Tel: 04 66 22 74 39
Tours available in German and English.

Association Kokopelli, Ales
www.kokopelli-seeds.com

Musée de l'Arles et de la Provence
www.arles-antique.org/mapa_cg13/root/index.htm
www.waterhistory.org/gallery/barbegal
Hours: March 1–October 31 every day,
9:00–19:00.
Tel: 04 90 18 88 88

Taberna Romana, Glanum
www.provence-prestige.tm.fr/boutiques/
taberna_romana/index_us
Hours: Open in the summer. Call for hours.
Tel: 04 90 92 65 97

Musée Camarguais
Parc Naturel Régional de Camargue
Mas du Pont de Rousty
Tel: 04 90 97 10 82

Musée du Riz en Camargue, Le Sambuc
Hours: Every day, 9:00–12:00 and
13:30–17:30.
Tel: 04 90 97 29 44

La Bastide de La Cabrière
Tel: 04 94 48 04 31

**Restaurant Maurin des Maures,
Rayol de Canadel**
Hours: Call to book.
Tel: 04 94 05 60 11

Hotel Restaurant Coteau Fleuri, Grimaud
www.coteaufleuri.fr/hotel.asp
Tel: 04 94 43 20 17

**Musée des Arts et Traditions Populaires,
Draguignan**
15 rue Joseph Roumanille
Hours: Closed Sunday morning and
Monday. Otherwise, 9:00–12:00 and
14:00–18:00.
Tel: 04 94 47 05 72

Apiculture Mandard, Draguignan
Tel: 04 94 68 05 10

Moulin de Callas, Callas
Tel: 04 94 39 03 20

Musée Escoffier de l'Art Culinaire, Villeneuve-Loubet
www.fondation-escoffier.org/
Hours: Every day except Monday, 14:00–18:00 in winter, 14:00–19:00 in summer.
Closed all November and on holidays.
Tel: 04 93 20 80 51

Musée Ethnographique de l'Olivier, Cagnes
Hours: Every day except Tuesdays and holidays, 10:00–12:00 and 14:00–17:00 (18:00 in summer). Closed much of November.
Tel: 04 93 20 85 57

Restaurant Escalinada, Nice
22 rue Pairolière
Tel: 04 93 62 11 71

La Citronneraie, Menton
Tel: 04 93 35 43 43

Musée du Terroir du Peille
Hours: Open weekend afternoons. Stop at the Mairie (Town Hall) to get entry.
Tel: 04 93 91 71 71

Les Violettes d'Yvette, Tourrettes-sur-Loup
Route des Costes
Tel: 04 93 59 28 49

Confiserie Florian, Pont du Loup
Le Pont du Loup
Hours: Free guided visits every day, including Sundays and public holidays, 9:00–12:00 and 14:00–18:30.
Tel: 04 93 59 32 91

Maison de Produits du Pays de Haute Provence
Route de Salagon
Hours: Open every day, 10:00–18:00; 10:00–19:00 on Saturdays.

Ecomusée des Pigeonniers de Haute-Provence at Le Moulin Fortune Arizzi, Les Bourelles
Le Mas des Pins
Hours: Phone ahead to see the pigeon house.
Tel: 04 92 34 04 80

La Thomassine Biodiversity Center, Manosque
Hours: July–September, Wednesday–Sunday, 10:30–17:00
Tel: 04 92 87 74 40

Le Musée de la Boulangerie, Bonnieux
12 rue de la République
Hours: Open daily except Tuesday.
July 1–August 31, 10:00–13:00 and 15:00–18:30
Tel: 04 90 75 88 34

Isle sur Sorgues
1 Avenue du Partage des Eaux
Tel: 04 90 20 77 37

Musée du Tire-Bouchon, Menerbes
Domaine de la Citadelle
Hours: Open every day April 1–October 31, 10:00–12:00, 14:00–19:00. Closed Sundays.
Tel: 04 90 72 41 58

Hôtel Restaurant Colombet
53 Place de la Libération, Nyons
Tel: 04 75 26 03 66

Institut du Monde de l'Olivier
Institute: 40 Place de la Liberation
Tel: 04 75 26 90 90
Museum: Place Olivier-de-Serres
Museum hours: Monday–Saturday, 15:00–18:00, during the season.
Tel: 04 75 26 12 12

Les Vieux Moulins
4 Promenade de la Digue
Hours: July–August, every day except Sunday afternoon, 10:00–12:00 and 14:30–18:00.
Tel: 04 75 26 11 00

La Scourtinerie
36, La Maladrerie
Hours: Monday–Friday, 9:30–12:00 and 14:00–18:00.
Tel: 04 75 26 33 52

Centre de ressources du Domaine Olivier de Serres, Mirabel
Tel: 04 75 36 30 58

Nougaterie Arnaud Soubeyran
Southern Industrial Zone
Hours: Monday–Saturday, 8:30–12:00 and 14:00–18:00.
Tel: 04 75 51 01 35

Le Chaudron d'Or, Montélimar
7, avenue du 52ème RI, Montélimar
Tel: 04 75 01 03 95

East

La Halle
Lyon
102, Crs Lafayette
Hours: Open every day except Monday and
Sunday afternoon, 7:00–12:00 and
15:00–19:00.

Brillat-Savarin birthplace, Belley
62, la Grande Rue

Bourg en Bresse Tourism Office
Centre Albert Camus
6 avenue Alsace Lorraine
Tel: 04 74 22 49 40

Le Hameau du Vin, Romaneche-Thorins
Tel: 03 85 35 22 22

**Maison du Blé et du Pain, Verdun sur le
Doubs**
Hours: Open every day, May 15–September
30, 15:00–19:00; 14:00–18:00 the rest of the
year.
Tel: 03 85 91 57 09

**Musée de la Vigne et du Vin, Beaune
(Burgundy Wine Museum)**
Hours: Open daily, 9:30–18:00; closed
Tuesdays.

La Moutarderie Fallot, Beaune
Hours: All visits must be in a group, maximum twenty people, arranged through the
Beaune Tourism Office—Tel: 03 80 26 21
30 or Email: contacts@ot-beaune.fr.
Note: You can visit just the museum or
combine it with a tour of the current production site.

Cassissium, Nuits St Georges
rue des Frères Montgolfier
www.cassissium.com
Hours: Open every day April 1–November
19, 10:00–13:00pm and 14:00–19:00.
Tel: 03 80 62 49 70

Maison du Comté, Poligny
Avenue de la Résistance, Poligny
Hours: Tuesday–Friday, 14:00–17:00.
Tel: 03 84 37 23 51

Arbois Cooperative Fromagerie
Hours: Open daily 8:00–12:00 and
17:30–19:30, closed Sunday afternoon.

Musée de la Vigne et du Vin, Arbois
Hours: Open every day July and August,
10:00–12:30 and 14:00–18:00.
Tel: 03 84 66 40 45

Maison de Louis Pasteur, Arbois
83, rue de Courcelles
Hours: Guided tours April 1–October 15,
every day at 9:45, 10:45, 11:45 and every 30
minutes from 14:15 to 18:15.
Tel: 03 84 66 11 72

Saline Royale, Arc et Senans
www.salineroyale.com
Hours: July–August, every day, 9:00–19:00.
Tel: 03 81 54 45 45

Distillerie Armand Guy, Pontparlier
www.pontarlier-anis.com
Hours: Tuesday–Saturday, 8–12, 14–18.
Tel: 03 81 39 04 70

Musée des Maisons Comtoises, Nancray
www.maisons-comtoises.org
Hours: April–October, every day,
10:00–19:00.
Tel: 03 81 55 29 77

Northeast

Ecomusée d'Alsace, Ungersheim
Hours: July and August, 9:30–19:00.
Tel: 03 89 74 44 74

**Musée du Vignoble et des Vins d'Alsace,
Kientzheim**
Hours: June 1–October 31, daily,
10:00–12:00 and 14:00–18:00.
Tel: 03 89 78 21 36

Maison du Pain d'Alsace, Selestat
www.maisondupain-d-alsace.com/
rue de Sel
Hours: July and August, Tuesday–Friday,
10:00–6:00; Saturday and Sunday,
10:00–5:00.
Tel: 03 88 58 45 90

**Musée du Pain d'Epices et des Douceurs
d'Autrefois, Gertwiller**
Place de la Mairie
Hours: July 1–September 15, Monday,
Wednesday, Friday, 14:00–18:00; Tuesday
and Thursday, 9:00–12:00 and 14:00–18:00.
Tel: 03 88 08 93 52

Maison de la Mirabelle, Rozelieures
16 rue du Capitaine Durand
Hours: May 1–October 31, daily except
Sunday, 9:00–11:00 and 13:30–17:30;
Sundays, 13:30-17:30.
Tel: 03 83 72 32 26

Confitures á la Lorraine, Bar-le-Duc
53 rue de l'Etoile
Tel: 03 29 79 06 81

Musée Européene de la Biére, Stenay
Hours: Open daily except Tuesdays, April
1-October 31. 10-18.
Tel: 03 29 80 68 78

Le Phare de Verzenay en Champagne, Verzenay
rue du Phare
51360 Verzenay
www.lepharedeverzenay.com/
Hours: Daily, 9:30–17:00; Saturday and Sunday to 17:30.
Tel: 03 26 07 87 87

You can visit many Champagne houses and caves in the region—one that provides a bit more, including another champagne museum, is Maison Launois Pere et Fils in Le Mesnil sur Oger. For the price of admission you can tour the cellars, explore a huge collection of Champagne memorabilia, and try three different champagnes. The guided tour lasts two hours. www.champagne-launois.fr/menu_musee.html

Le Musée des Temps Barbares et Ses Journées Merovingiennes, Marle
rue des Moulins
Hours: April 15–October 15, 14:00–19:00.
Tel: 03 23 24 01 33

Maison de la Chicorée, Orchies
25 rue Jules Roch
Hours: Call for hours.
Tel: 03 20 64 83 70

Musée de la Vie Rural, Steenwerck
Steenwerck
49 rue de Musée
Tel: 03 28 49 94 78. Phone for hours.

Ecomusée du Bommelaers Wall, Ghyvelde
Ghyvelde
20 route de Furnes
Hours: April 1–October 31,
Monday–Saturday, 10:00–18:00; Sundays,
14:00–18:00.
Tel: 03 28 20 11 03

Northwest

Mareis—Centre de la Pêche Artisanale, Etaples
Tel: 03 21 09 04 00

Palais Bénédictine, Fécamp
110 rue Alexandre le Grand
www.benedictine.fr/anglais/
Hours: Closed January. Summer hours, mid-July to early September, 10:00–18:00.
Otherwise, closed 12:00–14:00.
Tel: 33 02 35 10 26 10

Le Domaine St. Hippolyte, Lisieux
St Martin de la Lieue,
Hours: May 1–September 30, every day, 10:00–18:00.
Tel: 02 31 31 30 68

Le Père Jules, Saint-Desir-de Lisieux
Hours: Open every day. Call to arrange a group tour.
Tel: 02 31 14 57

La Ferme Président, Camembert
www.president.fr/franc/prod/histoir/moul_hist.htm

Isigny-Sainte-Mère Butter Factory
2, rue du Docteur Boutrois.
www.isigny-ste-mere.com/english/pages/Visite/visite.asp
Hours: Tours in July and August, Monday–Saturday at 10:00, 11:00, 14:00, 15:00, and 16:00. Otherwise, phone for an appointment.
Tel: 02 31 51 33 88.

Musée Regional du Cidre, Valognes
rue du Petit Versailles
Hours: July and August, open every day except Sunday morning, 10:00–12:00 and 14:00–18:00. Closed Tuesdays and Sunday mornings from April 1 to October 1.
Tel: 03 23 40 22 73

Epicerie Gosselin, St Vaast la Hogue
rue de Verrue
Hours: Tours, with the entertaining Bertrand Besselievre, must be arranged in advance.
Tel: 02 33 54 40 06

Restaurant de la Mere Poulard, Mont St Michel
www.mere-poulard.fr/restaurant.asp

Musée de la Fraise et du Patrimonie—Plougastel
www.musee-fraise.org/fr/index.htm
Near the church in the heart of Plougastel.
Hours: July–August, Monday–Friday, 10:00–12:30, 14:00–8:30; Saturday and Sunday, 14:00–18:30.

Biscuiterie François Garrec, Benodet
Route de Fouesnant
Hours: Daily visits Monday–Friday, 9:00–16:00.
Tel: 02 98 57 17 17

Musée de la Pêche, Concarneau
3 rue Vauban,
Tel: 02 98 97 10 20

Terre de Sel
Hours: Open July–August, every day, 9:30–12:30 and 14:30–19:00.
Tel: 02 40 62 08 80

Musée des Marais Salants, Batz sur Mer
29 bis, rue Pasteur
Hours: Open June 1–September 30, every day, 10:00–12:00 and 15:00–19:00.
Tel: 02 40 23 82 79

Maison des Paludiers, Saille
Tel: 02 40 62 21 96

Maison de la Mytiliculture, Tréhiguier
rue du Port Tréhiguier
Hours: Open daily July and August,
10:30–12:30 and 15:00–18:00.
Tel: 02 23 10 03 00

West

Le Moulin de la Falaise, Batz sur Mer
Hours: April 1–October 1, daily except
Sunday, 14:30–18:30.
Tel: 02 40 23 72 46

Biscuiterie des Marais
route du Croisic
Guérande
Hours: Open every day, all day.

Espace Escargots, Le Croisic
rue des Becs Sales.
www.espace-escargots.com/home.html
Hours: Open April–September, every day,
10:00–12:00 and 14:00–18:00.
Tel: 02 40 15 79 69

**Le Musée des Ustensiles de Cuisine
Ancien, St Denis la Chevasse**
Place Georges Clemenceau
Hours: Open July 1–September 15, every
day except Tuesday, 14:30–18:30.
Tel: 02 51 41 39 01

**Le Potager Extraordinaire,
La Mothe Achard**
Hours: Open daily, June 12–October 17;
July and August, 10:30–19:00.
Tel: 02 51 46 67 83

La Maison de la Mytiliculture, Esnandes
rue de l'Ocean
Hours: Open June 15–September 15, every
day, 10 30–12 30 and 14:00–19:00.
Tel: 05 46 01 34 64

Le Musée des Arts du Cognac, Cognac
Place de la Salle Verte
Hours: Open May 1–September 30, every
day, 10:00–18:00.
Tel: 05 45 32 07 25

Musée des Vins, Bordeaux
41 rue Borie
Tel: 05 57 87 50 60

Vinorama de Bordeaux, Bordeaux
12 cours du Médoc
Tel: 05 56 39 39 20

Château Mouton-Rothschild, Pauillac
Tel: 05 56 73 21 29

Oh! Légumes Oubliés, Sadirac
http://www.ohlegumesoublies.com
Groups are welcome for guided tours and
tastings, by appointment only.
Hours: Monday–Friday, 8:30–12:30 and
13:30–17:30
Tel: 05 56 30 61 00

Southwest

Le Musée Basque, Bayonne
37 Quai des Corsaires
www.musee-basque.com/fr/sommaire.asp
Hours: Closed Mondays and holidays.
Open May–October, 10:00–18:30; and
November 2–April 10, 12:30, 14:00–18:00.
Tel: 05 59 46 61 90

Chocolat Casenave, Bayonne
19, Arceaux du Port-Neuf
Tel: 05 59 59 03 16

Musée du Chocolat, Biarritz
14, avenue Beau Rivage.
www.lemuseeduchocolat.com/visite.html
Hours: Open July and August, every day,
10:00–18:00. Otherwise, open Monday to
Saturday.
Tel: 05 59 41 54 64

Le Musée du Gateau Basque, Sare
Quartier Lehenbiscay
www.legateaubasque.com
Tel: 05 59 54 22 09. Phone for hours.

Le Piment dans le Monde
Hours: Monday–Friday, 8:30–12:30,
14:00–18:00; Saturday, 9:30–12:30.

Route du Fromage for Brebis cheese
www.jambon-de-bayonne.com/site/pages/
maison/musee-1.htm

**La Maison du Jambon de Bayonne,
Arzacq**
Hours: Open July–August, every day,
10:00–13:00 and 14:30–18:30. Otherwise,
closed Sunday morning and Monday.
Tel: 05 59 04 49 35

Brasserie de Berry, Pau
4 rue Gachet

Maison de Cassoulet, Castelnaudry
24, Cours de la Republique
Tel: 04 68 23 27 23

Musée du Miel, Gramont
Tarn-et-Garonne
www.beekeeping.com/musee-du-miel/
Hours: Closed Wednesdays. Open June
1–September 30, 10:00–12:00 and
14:00–19:00.
Tel: 05 63 94 00 20

Musée de l'Armagnac, Condom
Anciennes Ecuries de l'Eveche
2, rue Jules Ferry
Hours: Closed Tuesdays and holidays.
Summer hours: daily, 10:00–12:00 and
15:00–18:00.
Tel: 05 62 28 31 41

Musée du Pruneau, Granges-sur-Lot
Hours: Open April-October, every day,
9:00–12:00, 14:00–19:00. Sundays and holidays, 15:00–19:00.
Tel: 05 53 84 00 69

Musée de Foie Gras, Frespech
www.souleilles-foiegras.com/musee
Hours: Summer, 10:00–19:00.
Tel: 05 53 41 23 24

**Cuzels Musée de Plein Air du Quercy,
Sauliac sur Cele, Lot**
Hours: Closed Saturdays. Open from April
to August. April, May, September, October:
14:00–18:00. June, 9:30–18:30. July and
August, 10:00–19:00.
Tel: 05 65 22 58 63

Pech-Merle Cave, Cabrerets
www.quercy.net/pechmerle/index.html

Musée Eclaté, Cardaillac
Hours: Guided tours in July and August,
every day except Saturday, at 15:00 and
16:30. September, 15:00 only. Any other
time, by appointment.
Tel: 05 65 40 10 63

La Borie d'Imbert, Rocamadour
Hours: Open April 1–September 30, every
day, 10:00-18:30.
Tel: 05 65 38 87 76

**Ecomusée de la Noix du Périgord,
Castelnaud-la-Chapelle**
Hours: Open April 1–November 1, every
day, 10:00 to 19:00. Also open by appoint-
ment, or by chance.
Tel: 05 53 59 69 63

Musée Vivant de l'Oie—Collonges la Rouge
Hours: Closed January. Open
April–August, every day, 10:00–12:30 and
14:00–19:00.
Tel: 05 55 84 03 40

**B&B run by Cathy and Alain Sarrazin in
Azay-le-Rideau**
9, Chemin des Cves, 37190 Azay le Rideau
www.sorges-perigord.com/ecomusegb.htm
Tel: 02 47 45 31 25

Center West

Ecomusée de la Truffe, Sorges
Hours: Open mid-June to mid-September,
every day, 9:30–12:30; mid-November to
February, every day except Monday,
14:00–17:00. Closed January 1, May 1,
November 1, and December 25.
Tel: 05 53 05 90 11

Maison de La Pomme d'Or, Lanouaille
4, place Thomas Robert Bugeaud
Hours: Open July 1–August 31, weekdays,
10:00–12 30 and 14:00–18 30.
Closed Saturday and Sunday
Tel: 05-53-62-17-82

Le Musée de la Boucherie, Limoges
rue de la Boucherie
Hours: Open July–September, daily,
10:00–13:00 and 15:00–19:00.

**Château de la Bourdaisière,
Montlouis sur Loire**
25, rue de la Bourdaisière
Montlouis sur Loire

Château Villandry
www.chateauvillandry.com/
Hours: Open July 1–February 29, 9:00–17:30.
Tel: 02 47 50 02 09

L'Etape Gourmande, Villandry
L'Etape Gourmande "La Giraudière"
Villandry
www.letapegourmande.com/indexen.html
Tel: 02 47 50 08 60

La Poire Tapée à l'Ancienne, Quincay
www.poirestapees.com/frames.html
Hours: Open every day, 10:00–12:00 and
14:00–19:00.
Tel: 02 47 95 45 19. Phone for group events.

Musée du Champignon, Saumur
www.musee-du-champignon.com/#ppres

**La Maison de Tante Léonie
Musée Marcel Proust, Illiers-Combray**
Hours: Closed Mondays and December
15–January 15. Open July 2–August 31,
tours at 11:00, 14:30, and 16:00.
Tel: 02 37 24 30 97

La Ferme Médiévale de Bois Richeux
www.meridies.org/as/dmir/Herbal/1408.html.
Hours: Open July 1–14, Tuesday–Friday,
10:00–12:00 and 14:00–18:00. July
15–August 31, every day except Monday.
Tel: 06 11 88 20 20

COMPA, Chartres
Pont de Mainvilliers, 28000 Chartres
Hours: Closed Mondays. Open
Tuesday–Friday, 10:00–12:30 and 13:30–18:00.
Saturdays and Sundays until 19:00.
Tel: 02 37 84 15 00e Gourm

Index of Subjects

Acknowledgements

The idea for this book was born when Ib Bellew and Carole Kitchel of Bunker Hill Publishing zipped through the Musée du Jambon in Arzacq. Taken with the idea that if a ham museum exists, then food museums must abound in France, they found The FOOD Museum on the Internet and asked us to write about the food museums of France. Thank you, Ib and Carole—it's been a tasty ride.

Thanks also to Louise O'Brien at Maison de la France, the French Tourism Office based in New York, for her help in unleashing tourism ladies and a few gentlemen across France who so generously opened so many doors.

We salute, too, the inn keepers, museum personnel, purveyors, farmers, gardeners, hoteliers, chefs, restaurant owners, shop keepers and others who told us their stories and guided us to more. Special thanks to Benoît Thevenet of Nyons, and Margaret Fountain Smith of Vermont, who wrestled our business cards and explanatory hand-outs into respectable formal French.

We are grateful also to Rick Zednik and Rachel Hammonds, and Roswitha and Fred Gans, in whose homes we finished the final part of the book.

And to illustrator Sally Maddox. Her graceful maps illuminate our journey.

And finally, special love and appreciation to our son Gulliver, a university student and avid traveler, who capably took care of hearth and home for us while we were away.

Picture Credits

Tom Hughes photos: Cover, pp.13-15, 17, 19, 21-33, 35-46, 48, 49, 51-61, 65-68, 72-75, 77-78, 81, 83-87, 89, 90, 92-98, 100-107, 108-110, 115-118, 120.

The FOOD Museum Collection: pp. 9-12, 15-19, 27-28, 42, 44-45, 48, 50, 52, 54, 56, 62-65, 67-70, 73, 76, 79-81, 83, 85, 91, 96, 104, 111, 113, 114, 117, 119, 120.

Draguignan Museum, p34; Comté Cheese, p60; **Maison du Johnnies**, p80; **Les Huitres d'Ile de Ré**, p88.

All maps by Sally Maddox.

No More Moules
by Frances Wells

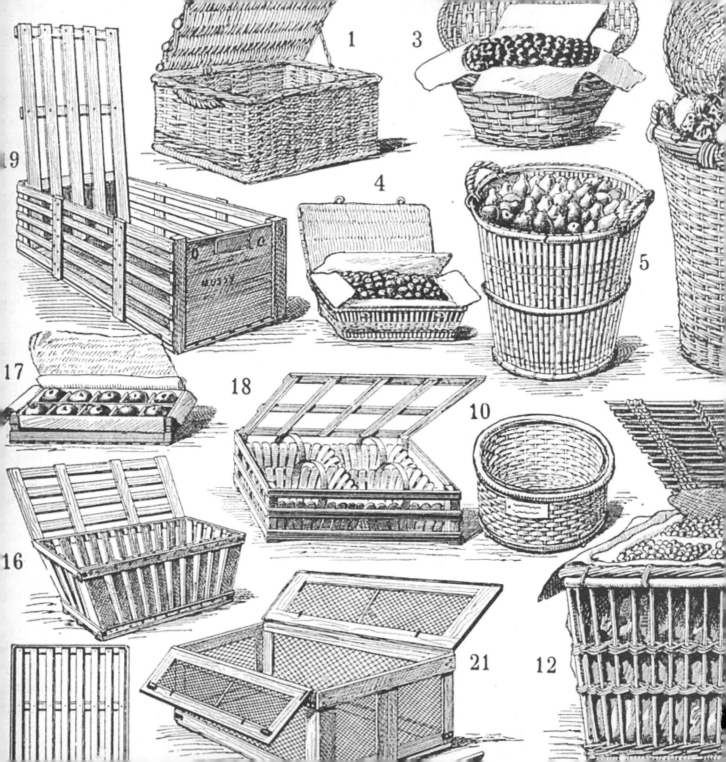